## The Thirteen Colonies

# Pennsylvania

### Victoria Sherrow

Lucent Books, Inc.
10911 Technology Place, San Diego, California 92127

*On Cover: Landing of William Penn*

Library of Congress Cataloging-in-Publication Data

Sherrow, Victoria.
    Pennsylvania / by Victoria Sherrow.
        p. cm. — (The thirteen colonies)
Includes bibliographical references and index.
    ISBN 1-56006-993-7 (alk. paper)
    1. Pennsylvania—History—Colonial period, ca. 1600–1775—Juvenile
literature. 2. Pennsylvania—History—1775–1865—Juvenile literature.
[1. Pennsylvania—History—1775–1865.] I. Title. II. Thirteen colonies
(Lucent Books).
    F152 .S56 2002
    974.8'02—dc21

2001003195

Copyright 2002 by Lucent Books, Inc.
an imprint of the Gale Group
10911 Technology Place, San Diego, California 92127

Printed in the U.S.A.

# Contents

# Foreword

T he story of the thirteen English colonies that became the United States of America is one of startling diversity, conflict, and cultural evolution. Today, it is easy to assume that the colonists were of one mind when fighting for independence from England and afterwards when the national government was created. However, the American colonies had to overcome a vast reservoir of distrust rooted in the broad geographical, economic, and social differences that separated them. Even the size of the colonies contributed to the conflict; the smaller states feared domination by the larger ones.

These sectional differences stemmed from the colonies' earliest days. The northern colonies were more populous and their economies were more diverse, being based on both agriculture and manufacturing. The southern colonies, however, were dependent on agriculture—in most cases, the export of only one or two staple crops. These economic differences led to disagreements over things such as the trade embargo the Continental Congress imposed against England during the war. The southern colonies wanted their staple crops to be exempt from the embargo because their economies would have collapsed if they could not trade with England, which in some cases was the sole importer. A compromise was eventually made and the southern colonies were allowed to keep trading some exports.

In addition to clashing over economic issues, often the colonies did not see eye to eye on basic political philosophy. For example, Connecticut leaders held that education was the route to greater political liberty, believing that knowledgeable citizens would not allow themselves to be stripped of basic freedoms and rights. South Carolinians, on the other hand, thought that the protection of personal property and economic independence was the basic foundation of freedom. In light of such profound differences it is amazing that the colonies were able to unite in the fight for independence and then later under a strong national government.

Why, then, did the colonies unite? When the Revolutionary War began the colonies set aside their differences and banded together because they shared a common goal—gaining political freedom from what they considered a tyrannical monarchy—that could be more easily attained if they cooperated with each other. However, after the war ended, the states abandoned unity and once again pursued sectional interests, functioning as little nations in a weak confederacy. The congress of this confederacy, which was bound by the Articles of Confederation, had virtually no authority over the individual states. Much bickering ensued—the individual states refused to pay their war debts to the national government, the nation was sinking further into an economic depression, and there was nothing the national government could do. Political leaders realized that the nation was in jeopardy of falling apart. They were also aware that European nations such as England, France, and Spain were all watching the new country, ready to conquer it at the first opportunity. Thus the states came together at the Constitutional Convention in order to create a system of government that would be both strong enough to protect them from invasion and yet nonthreatening to state interests and individual liberties.

The Thirteen Colonies series affords the reader a thorough understanding of how the development of the individual colonies helped create the United States. The series examines the early history of each colony's geographical region, the founding and first years of each colony, daily life in the colonies, and each colony's role in the American Revolution. Emphasis is given to the political, economic, and social uniqueness of each colony. Both primary and secondary quotes enliven the text, and sidebars highlight personalities, legends, and personal stories. Each volume ends with a chapter on how the colony dealt with changes after the war and its role in developing the U.S. Constitution and the new nation. Together, the books in this series convey a remarkable story—how thirteen fiercely independent colonies came together in an unprecedented political experiment that not only succeeded, but endures to this day.

# Introduction

# "The Seed of a Nation"

Although Pennsylvania was nearly the last of the thirteen original colonies to be founded, it became the third most populous and one of the most prosperous and influential. Drawn by Pennsylvania's favorable geographical features and unique political system, people from diverse backgrounds came together to live, work, and govern themselves in ways that helped to shape their new homeland and to create their new identity as "Americans."

From the beginning, Pennsylvania's founder offered people religious freedom. As a member of the Society of Friends, or Quakers, William Penn had endured religious persecution in England, where he was even imprisoned for his religious practices. Groups that were ostracized, ridiculed, or even banned in their homelands could live in Pennsylvania. There, they would not be attacked or arrested for attending their own religious services or for refusing to pay taxes to support a government-sponsored church. They would not be outcasts because they chose to think differently than their leaders. Religious liberty was a new experience for most settlers, but the idea took root and became central to American law and part of the First Amendment to the U.S. Constitution.

Penn was a practical man as well as an idealist, and he wanted his colony to grow and prosper. To attract people with various skills and talents, he advertised his colony throughout Europe, describing

Pennsylvania's rich soil, fine river systems, and other attractions. In addition, by selling land at relatively low prices, he made it possible for more people to buy land in his colony. Most of these new settlers were middle- and lower-class people—farmers, laborers, craftsmen, and merchants who had never been landowners before—along with a minority of wealthy people and aristocrats. Many newcomers were so

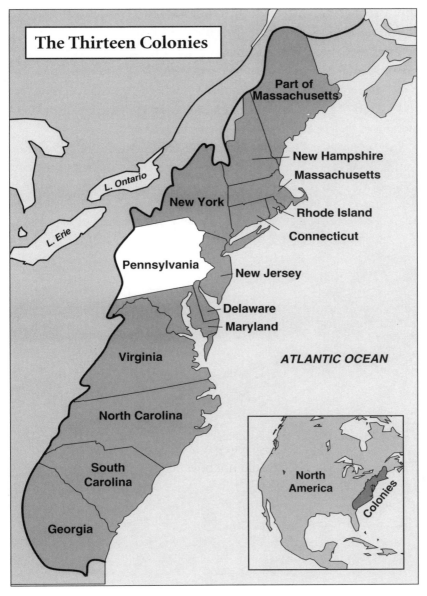

## The Thirteen Colonies

Part of Massachusetts

New Hampshire

Massachusetts

L. Ontario

New York

Rhode Island

Connecticut

L. Erie

Pennsylvania

New Jersey

Delaware

Maryland

Virginia

ATLANTIC OCEAN

North Carolina

South Carolina

North America

Colonies

Georgia

poor that they arrived as indentured servants obligated to work for a certain number of years to earn their freedom. These factors combined to make Pennsylvanians an unusually diverse mixture of people who valued their new freedoms and were willing to work hard to succeed.

Believing that his colony would not thrive unless people had confidence in their government, Penn offered people basic civil rights and a chance to participate in the lawmaking process. From the beginning, colonists elected representatives to an assembly that made and approved new laws. As head of the colony, Penn changed the governmental structure over time so that people steadily gained more rights. The colonists became accustomed to the idea of self-government, and a form of grassroots leadership evolved in Pennsylvania that later influenced the government of the new United States.

Similarly, a strong sense of justice motivated Penn's relationship with Native Americans. Penn said they were entitled to the rights whites enjoyed, including trial by jury. He refused to take land by force and told

William Penn, head of the colony of Pennsylvania, established a peaceful relationship with the Native Americans, one that lasted for seventy years.

his agents not to exploit or enslave the Indians. As a result, the Indians trusted Penn and helped the early white settlers to survive in their new homeland. For seventy years the two groups lived together peacefully, a situation that was unique among the colonies and that further enhanced growth and economic development.

From the moment he envisioned a diverse colony offering religious freedom, William Penn knew that he faced many challenges, but he hoped that his colonists would live in harmony and that Pennsylvania would prosper. He said, "'Tis a clear and just thing, and my God that has given it me through many difficultys [sic], will, I believe bless and make it the seed of a nation."[1]

The colony continued to grow during the eighteenth century, becoming more populous and even more diverse as new settlers arrived. The freedom-loving people who came to Pennsylvania contributed their individual talents and played major roles in building their communities and, later, a new nation. The colony's abundant agriculture fed colonists throughout America, and its factories produced vital raw materials and products people used at home and at work. Having experienced oppression themselves, many Pennsylvanians also felt compelled to help others. A group in Germantown took the lead in the abolition movement that would swell during the late eighteenth and early nineteenth centuries when they made the first formal protests against slavery, the antithesis of freedom.

Likewise, as the colonists moved toward independence from their British rulers, Pennsylvania played a key role. In Philadelphia, which had become the largest and most important colonial city, newspapers published spirited articles favoring independence that were read all over the thirteen colonies. It was in Philadelphia that Thomas Paine published his stirring pamphlet, *Common Sense*, which persuaded many Americans to take a firm stand for independence. Delegates from the colonies met in Philadelphia for the Continental Congresses, in which they declared themselves a free and independent nation. And though the colony was founded by Quakers, who oppose war and violence, many Pennsylvanians were active in the fight for freedom.

After the war, once again the nation's leaders met in Philadelphia for the Constitutional Convention of 1787, during which they wrote the laws and a plan for the new U.S. government. From 1790 to 1800,

Philadelphia served as the nation's capital from 1790 to 1800, and was home to the First Bank of the United States, built on Third Street.

Philadelphia served as the nation's capital and was the location of the First Bank of the United States and the U.S. Mint. The state of Pennsylvania was a center of political and intellectual activity, with a strong economy based on agriculture, industry, and trade. As America's first real melting pot, it demonstrated that people from diverse backgrounds could find ways to live together, despite religious and cultural differences.

# Chapter One

# A Welcoming Land

The people who settled present-day Pennsylvania found a hospitable region with abundant natural resources. It provided them with water, food, and the materials they could use for shelter, clothing, tools, and household goods.

The land is made up of mountains, hills, plateaus, and valleys—as diverse as the people who would settle there. Before Europeans arrived, about 90 percent of Pennsylvania was covered with forests rich in both hardwood and softwood trees. Deer, elks, bison, black bears, moose, and wolves roamed the region, as did raccoons, otters, beavers, rabbits, woodchucks, foxes, and wildcats. The southeast is a fertile region with rolling hills and valleys.

Lakes, streams, and three major river systems provide another vital resource. One of these systems connects Pennsylvania with the Atlantic Ocean; another flows into the Mississippi, North America's longest river. The Delaware River, which flows in eastern Pennsylvania, stretches south from New York's Catskill Mountains for about 375 miles, then empties into the Delaware Bay and the Atlantic Ocean south of Philadelphia. Three other rivers—the Lackawanna, Lehigh, and Schuylkill—enter the Delaware. These rivers naturally attracted settlers, offering them sources of freshwater and a means to transport people and goods—something that particularly interested the Europeans who began arriving in the 1600s.

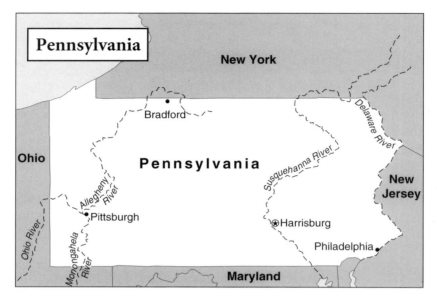

## Living Off the Land

Different groups of Native Americans lived in present-day Pennsylvania for at least twelve thousand years before Europeans arrived. By the 1600s several tribal groups lived in Pennsylvania. The largest were the Leni-Lenape, which means "Real Men" or "Men of Our Nation." They were part of the Algonquian group that included many tribes on the Atlantic Coast. Groups of Leni-Lenape lived along the Delaware River, which they called the Lenape. Other Algonquian groups in the region were the Conoy, Nanticoke, and Shawnee. Monongahela Indians lived in western Pennsylvania. Another group, the Erie, were related to the Iroquois, a powerful group that lived primarily in New York.

Indians in this region were hunters, gatherers, and farmers who tended to live in settled communities instead of moving from place to place. Groups of farming Indians formed villages in which they lived according to their laws and customs. Using the materials in their surroundings, the Leni-Lenape and some other groups built longhouses—rectangular houses with curved roofs shingled with elm bark—or wigwams, circular dwellings made of bent saplings covered with hides or bark. Longhouses could hold five families of the same clan. Fire pits for each family were built at intervals of about twenty feet, with a smoke hole in the ceiling above each pit.

Native peoples spent a great deal of their time producing, preserving, and storing food. Each spring, women planted crops, including maize (Indian corn), squash, pumpkins, sweet potatoes, and beans. In addition to farming, hunting was another important way to obtain food. The men used spears and nets to catch herring, shad, and other fish, and they caught wild ducks, geese, and swans for food. Spring was also the time to collect maple sap from the trees and to boil it down to make syrup and sugar.

During late summer and fall, men spent more time hunting deer and bears for meat and also for skins. They also hunted beavers and otters, two small fur-bearing animals that were plentiful in the region. This was also the time to harvest crops. Maize was a particularly important crop and could be used in many ways, either fresh or dried and ground up in the form of meal. The villagers also gathered edible berries, mushrooms,

The Leni-Lenape people, the largest tribal group living in Pennsylvania in the 1600s, lived in longhouses that could hold up to five families.

# Changes for Native Americans

Early white settlers faced many difficulties, and the Indians helped them to survive in their new environment. Native peoples taught the Europeans how to plant corn and other crops and how to preserve food for the winter.

Indians gradually changed their way of life and became more dependent on these newcomers. Through trade, they obtained tools, pots, and other items and stopped making these things for themselves. Whites also offered them guns and alcohol, which often caused problems because Indians had not traditionally consumed alcoholic beverages and were not used to the effects. In his book *Pennsylvania, Birthplace of a Nation*, historian Sylvester K. Stevens writes, "The typical white trader lived by his wits and drove the shrewdest possible bargain with the red man for his valuable firs. Rum was used all too frequently in this process. . . . It was the trader also who furnished the Indian with guns and the powder with which to fire them."

Many Indians died from the loss of food resources and from diseases. They had once used the land freely for hunting, fishing, and planting, but new settlers erected fences and other boundaries, depleted the natural resources, and took more and more land during the 1700s. Europeans also brought smallpox, measles, and other diseases that were new to North America. Indians were not immune to these diseases, and many of them died during epidemics.

Native Americans trade their furs for goods and supplies from early European settlers.

herbs, and roots from the woods and meadows, and they dried their vegetables and surplus meat and smoked fish for the winter. These were stored in deep pits, which were dug in the ground and lined with bark or grasses.

The cold months were a time to make and repair tools, utensils, and containers. The earth yielded clay, which was made into containers for cooking and storage. Using animal skins and furs, the people made clothing and blankets, adorning them with porcupine quills, shells, and other things from the land. With luck, the stored food would last all winter, but if supplies ran short, the men went hunting wearing snowshoes they fashioned from tree saplings.

The Indians traded with each other and sometimes traveled long distances for that purpose, using canoes made from hollowed-out tree trunks or pieces of elm bark to carry them across the water. During the 1600s they also began to trade with white Europeans who came to the region in search of furs and other goods.

## The First Europeans

Nobody knows for sure who was the first European to reach present-day Pennsylvania, but several European countries sent explorers to the Atlantic Coast during the early 1600s to find new trade routes and economic opportunities. In 1608 Captain John Smith sailed up the Susquehanna River and encountered some Susquehannock Indians before returning to Virginia, where he had already helped to found an English colony in Jamestown. However, the English did not send settlers to the Pennsylvania region or establish any trading posts at that time.

The next year Henry Hudson, an English explorer working for the Dutch, reached the mouth of the Lenape River. He did not find the water routes to Asia he had been seeking, but the Dutch government expressed an interest in the region after Hudson described its natural resources and waterways. He reported that the Indians "had an abundance of provisions, skins, and furs, of martens and foxes, and many other commodities, as birds and fruits, even white and red grapes."[2] The Dutch government saw promising trade opportunities.

The Delaware River was named after Thomas West, baron De La Warr, appointed lord governor of the Virginia Colony in 1609.

That same year Englishman Samuel Argall arrived and renamed the Lenape River the Delaware River after Thomas West, baron De La Warr, who had recently been appointed lord governor of the Virginia Colony. The English then gave the same name, Delaware, to the Leni-Lenape Indians they found living along the river. They began to think of this region as English territory, but they did not make specific plans to settle there.

Meanwhile, Holland coveted this region, too, and claimed it in 1613, calling it part of New Netherland, the Dutch colony in present-day New York. The Dutch sent traders down the Delaware River to offer the Indians cloth, metal cooking pans, knives, guns, tools, and glass beads in exchange for beaver pelts. Beaver pelts fetched high prices in Europe, where they were made into hats, muffs, and coat trimmings. Other countries also realized the lucrative trading opportunities in the region, and they founded settlements along with trading posts. For nearly half a century various European rulers would aspire to control the riches of the future Pennsylvania Colony.

## New Sweden

In 1637 a group of Dutch and Swedes hired Peter Minuit to organize a Swedish trading post in the region to obtain beaver pelts from local Indians. Minuit arrived the next spring with a hundred settlers from Sweden and Finland. When Minuit discovered Dutch families already living on the eastern shore of the Delaware, he took his group to the west bank near present-day Wilmington, Delaware, where they founded New Sweden and built Fort Christina, named in honor of the Swedish queen who had sponsored their voyage.

The Swedes developed a profitable fur trade with Delaware and Susquehannock Indians, and to protect their trading post from attacks by the Dutch and English who lived around them, the government wanted to build new, self-sustaining settlements in the region. More settlers would also help build the fur industry and harvest more lumber, which could be exported for cash. However, the Swedish government had trouble finding more people who wanted to leave Sweden for America, and New Sweden grew slowly.

In 1643, a group of the Swedish settlers did move from their community in present-day Delaware to found the first European settlement inside the borders of Pennsylvania. The New Sweden Company sent a new governor, Johan Printz, a clergyman's son and a Swedish military officer who was known for his efficiency and large size: over six feet tall and about four hundred pounds. Printz decided to relocate some of the settlers to Tinicum, an island in the Delaware River near the mouth of the Schuylkill. He thought an island would be safer from Dutch and English interference. A neighboring community was formed in Uppland (later renamed Chester), which is today also part of Pennsylvania. The governor expected that more settlers would join these groups and also settle the areas in between them, fortifying their settlements.

On Tinicum, the settlement of New Gothenburg, named for Gothenburg (or Göteborg), Sweden, served as a capital of New Sweden. The settlers of New Gothenburg included skilled carpenters and roofers. The Finns among them were experts at clearing forests, which were an excellent source of building materials but were also a hindrance because the land had to be cleared before settlers could grow their crops, which included winter grain, corn, and beans. In addition to removing trees and burning the stumps, settlers had to pull out certain roots that permeated the area and obstructed their plows. They did this job by hand with metal hoes.

Johan Printz (right) was made governor of New Sweden, the first European settlement inside the borders of Pennsylvania.

Soon they erected a fort, trading post, storehouse, cabins, and community buildings. Their fort contained four large brass cannons they had brought with them on the ship. These settlers also built the first courthouse, school, and church on Pennsylvania soil. Lutheran ministers taught children reading, writing, simple arithmetic, and religious concepts at Tinicum.

Nonetheless, the settlers experienced many difficulties during their first two years, and several people died from malnutrition. To prevent this from happening again, Governor Printz distributed regular food rations to his colonists until they were growing enough crops to sustain themselves. The settlers also learned better methods of growing crops from friendly Indians in the area, and their harvests improved in the following years.

In addition to building up the fur trade, Swedish rulers had instructed Printz to "cull choice woods from the forest," to raise "grain and other vegetables," and "to procure a good race of cattle, sheep and other animals."[3] Under the governor's stern leadership, the colonists succeeded in carrying out these tasks. He also established good relations with the Native Americans and dealt fairly with them, which helped to maintain the peace and to increase trade.

But Printz was continually frustrated by the lack of growth in the colony. He complained that Swedish leaders did not send enough settlers or support to defend the colony, which stretched across a large area of land. In 1647 Printz sent this report to officials in his homeland:

> The Fort in Skylenkyll, called Karsholm, is nearly ready. We are filling and working at it every day. So that, if we had people, ammunition, and other necessary resources, we should certainly not only be in a position to maintain ourselves in the said places, but also be enabled to settle and fortify other fine sites. Again, 28 freemen are settled, and part of them provided with oxen and cows, so that they already begin to prosper; but women are wanting. . . . The country is very well suited for all sorts of cultivation; also for whale fishery and wine, if some one was here who understood the business. Mines of silver and gold may possibly be discovered, but nobody here has any knowledge about such things.[4]

# The Practical Log Cabin

Swedes introduced to America the log cabin, a practical dwelling that did not require nails. Nearly all of the settlers of New Gothenburg lived in these cabins, which usually consisted of one room or one room with a loft at one end. The finest home in the settlement was the Printzhof, a large cedar log home with brick fireplaces where Governor Printz lived with his wife and six children.

Log cabins were constructed of hewn logs left in their natural rounded shape and designed to fit together with notches and pegs. Roofs were made from bark or bundles of straw or rushes, and a mixture of mud, wood chips, and moss was plugged into the cracks to keep the interior warm and dry. New settlers who saw the Swedish cabins carried the idea westward. Because the cabins required just one tool, an axe, and used naturally available materials, settlers could more easily construct dwellings on the frontier.

The log cabin, introduced to America by the Swedes, was popular in the 1700s because it could be constructed using only an axe.

By 1653 the population of the colony remained under two hundred people and the sixty-year-old Printz became so discouraged that he resigned his position and left for Europe. Printz turned over the governorship of New Sweden to his son-in-law, who was in charge until a new governor arrived. With so few colonists and few armaments to defend themselves, New Sweden was vulnerable to attacks from the neighboring Dutch, just as Printz had feared.

## A Coveted Region

Dutch settlers in New Netherland had observed the rich fur trade to the south with great interest. Their governor, Peter Stuyvesant, also knew that the Swedes hoped to expand and move into the surrounding areas, something he wanted to prevent. In 1653 Stuyvesant sent two hundred men to build Fort Casimir between the two Swedish forts on the Delaware River. He announced that he would not permit any expansion of the Swedish settlements.

The next year a new governor named Johan Rising took charge of New Sweden, and he decided to try to seize Fort Casimir from the Dutch. In response, an angry Peter Stuyvesant sent Dutch troops to seize the Swedish settlements. They surrendered without much of a fight, leaving the Dutch in control of the region and its lucrative fur trade.

However, the English were becoming increasingly powerful in the region. Colonists from England had already founded the first two permanent European settlements in America: Jamestown, Virginia, and Plymouth, Massachusetts. By 1628 they had added a colony in Massachusetts Bay and new settlements in Connecticut, New Hampshire, and Rhode Island, known collectively with Massachusetts as New England. In 1634 the English founded Maryland in the Chesapeake region, next to Virginia.

Now they sought to claim the lands between New England and Maryland. James, the duke of York and the brother of King Charles II, wanted England to hold all of the land between the Hudson and Delaware Rivers. James was both the commander of the British navy and the head of the Royal African Company, which hoped to gain control of the slave trade in the Americas. Their main rival in the slave trade was the Dutch West India Company, so by seizing Dutch territory in America they could not only dominate the slave trade but also control the fur trade and other resources. These lands, which included parts of the future Pennsylvania colony, held major rivers and ports on the Atlantic Coast.

In 1664 James sent British ships to America, where they claimed that New Netherland belonged to England. Although Stuyvesant wanted to open fire on the British, his fort was poorly equipped and he could not hope to win an armed struggle. As a result, for the next century the British controlled the whole region, except for a brief period in 1673 when the Dutch returned and held their former territory for a year. England's rulers now regarded this land as their property to use as they saw fit. Like the Native American inhabitants who preceded them, they would settle on the land and make use of its rivers, forests, wild game, and other abundant resources. In addition to these resources, the new colony of Pennsylvania would offer Europeans religious freedom and other rights they had not enjoyed in their homeland.

# Chapter Two

# William Penn's "Holy Experiment"

O n April 2, 1681, in one of the largest individual land grants in history, King Charles II granted Englishman William Penn the land between the fortieth and forty-third parallels and extending from the Delaware River to the Great Lakes. The grant later expanded to include present-day Delaware, known as the Lower Counties, which became a separate colony in 1702.

Even before he reached America himself, Penn thought carefully about how to govern his colony. He was determined to make it into a religious haven, not only for his fellow Quakers but also for others. Tolerance and the idea that each person had value in God's sight were fundamental to Penn's personal belief system, and they profoundly influenced his plan of government. In the words of historian David Freeman Hawke,

> Pennsylvania, more than any other English colony in America, was the lengthened shadow of a single man. William Penn blended the ideal and the practical to a fine balance. He envisioned a haven for the oppressed and also a prosperous colony to fatten his fortune. [5]

## A Quaker Leader

William Penn was born on October 14, 1644, into a life of wealth and privilege. His father, Admiral Sir William Penn, came from a respected old English family and was a naval hero. As a child, Penn received a fine education and was reared in the Anglican faith, like most other English aristocrats. England's rulers supported this church as the official religion of the land, but Penn found himself disagreeing with some of its principles as he grew older. He showed a strong interest in new religious ideas when he became a student at Oxford University. When he refused to conform to Anglican religious practices at the school and attended unauthorized prayer meetings, he was expelled.

Admiral Penn sent his son to a Protestant school in France, hoping that new friends and the pleasures of life abroad would distract William from his nonconformist ideas. When Penn returned to London, he proceeded to study law at Lion's Inn, then he went to supervise his

William Penn received the charter for Pennsylvania from King Charles II in 1681.

father's estates in Ireland in 1666. During the next year, Penn embraced a new religion after hearing the missionary Thomas Loe, a member of the Religious Society of Friends, or Quakers. Penn had first heard Loe speak when he was twelve years old, but this time Loe's message took firm root.

Quakers were persecuted in England because they refused to support wars or to fight in the military. Nor would they remove their hats or bow in the presence of royalty because they believed all people were equal in God's sight, something the royals regarded as traitorous. Quakers also refused to swear oaths to tell the truth in a court of law because the Bible said, "Thou shalt not swear" and because Quakers professed to be truthful at all times, making such oaths unnecessary. During the 1600s thousands of Quakers were arrested and imprisoned for offenses against the Crown or for preaching Quakerism or attending Quaker meetings.

Quakers were not popular in the developing American colonies, either. In Massachusetts and Connecticut, the Puritans, who had also been a minority in England, called them a "pernicious sect"[6] and passed laws against their religious activities. Two Quakers were hanged in Boston. Roger Williams, who grudgingly allowed Quakers to settle in his Rhode Island Colony, strongly disagreed with their pacifism and their belief in equality.

Penn became an outspoken Quaker leader and used his money and social position to help other Quakers. He also traveled throughout England speaking out against religious intolerance. In 1669 he was imprisoned for preaching and writing about his beliefs. Nonetheless, after his release Penn continued to express his ideas, even after he was jailed a second time. He said, "My prison shall be my grave before I will budge a jot."[7]

Eventually Penn became determined to build a Quaker colony in America. (George Fox, the founder of the Society of Friends, had visited North America in 1669 and had expressed the hope that his followers would find refuge there.) William Penn saw a way to make this hope a reality. Penn's father had died in 1670. King Charles II had borrowed money from Admiral Penn, and in 1680 Penn decided to ask that the loan be repaid in land rather than in money.

Penn received fifty thousand square miles of land west of the Delaware River. The next year the three lower counties on the Delaware were added

# A New Religion

Around 1647 George Fox founded a new Protestant religion known as the Society of Friends, or Quakers. Fox believed every person had value in God's sight and anyone could speak directly to God. At their services, called meetings, Quakers did not recite set prayers or sing hymns. Instead, they sat quietly and rose to speak if they had an insight to share with the group, and in keeping with their principle that no person was inherently superior to another, both men and women were free to express ideas.

The Friends espoused ideals of honesty, simplicity, and nonviolence. Their peace testimony was first set forth during the mid-seventeenth century, when the group declared their commitment against harming or killing another human being or supporting violent activities. In *A Portrait in Grey,* biographer John Punshon quotes Fox as saying in 1684 that "the Spirit of Christ that leads us into all Truth will never move us to fight and war against any man with outward weapons neither for the kingdom of Christ nor for the kingdoms of this world."

In 1647 George Fox founded the Society of Friends, later known as the Quakers. The group believed that every person could speak directly to God.

King Charles told William Penn to name his colony after his father, Admiral Sir William Penn (pictured).

to this grant. Under the terms of the charter, Pennsylvania was a proprietary colony, which meant that the Crown gave one individual—Penn—the authority to found and govern the colony and convey this power to his heirs. King Charles told Penn to name the colony after his father, but Penn preferred Silvania, which means "Woodlands," and thought it a sign of vanity to give the colony his family name. When Charles insisted, he added "Penn," and the name became Pennsylvania—"Penn's Woodlands."

## Planning the Government

William Penn called his colony a "Holy Experiment," where he would implement his ideas about how diverse people could live in harmony, according to his Quaker beliefs. He declared that Pennsylvania would be "a Commonwealth founded on the principal of brotherly Love ... which would stand above the differences in religion that every settlement was bound to display."[8]

Penn then put into writing the principles of government he hoped would foster brotherly love and prosperity. He believed that people would thrive if they had some voice in their own government, received equal treatment under the law, and also took responsibility for observing the laws. Pennsylvania's first constitution, the Frame of Government, took effect on May 5, 1682. It provided for religious liberty, an elected assembly, a free press, private property rights, and free enterprise. The frame stated that Pennsylvania would have a governor (Penn) with the power to appoint judges and preside over the seventy-two-man council, and a deputy governor. People eligible to vote would elect a legislature consisting of the council and a two hundred-man assembly to make laws, which the governor could veto. In order to vote, men must own land and believe in God.

The frame included a penal code that provided for trial by jury. Only two offenses—murder and treason—were punishable by death, starkly contrasting with England, where people could be hanged for about two hundred crimes at that time.

In a section called the Declaration of Rights, Penn declared that Pennsylvanians would be free to worship according to their own religious beliefs and that the state would not sponsor any particular religion over another. Colonists need never pay taxes that supported a religion or help build a religious structure against their will, nor would they be forced to pay ministers of a different faith. He wrote eloquently about freedom of religion, or "the rights of conscience," saying,

> All men have a natural and infeasible right to worship Almighty God according to the dictates of their own consciences; no man can of right be compelled to attend, erect, or support any place of worship, or to maintain any ministry against his consent; no human authority can, in any case whatever, control or interfere with the rights of conscience, and no preference shall ever be given by law to any religious establishment or modes of worship. [9]

Penn also discussed property rights and the right to hold diverse political opinions. He wrote, "Men being born with a title to perfect freedom and uncontrolled enjoyment of all the rights and privileges of the law of nature . . . no one can be put out of his estate and subjected to the political view of another, without his consent." [10]

Although he believed in some self-government, Penn worried that wealthy Englishmen might not invest in his colony if they thought the colonists had too much control. Penn wanted investors to buy land and send people, tools, and equipment to boost the economy. To appease potential investors,

In establishing the government of Pennsylvania, William Penn emphasized freedom of religion and wanted citizens to have a voice in the political system.

Penn appointed a deputy governor and a council of officials to act on his behalf. The council could make laws, but the colonial assembly could approve or reject them. This compromise took some power away from the elected assembly.

Late in 1681 Penn wrote to the settlers who already lived in the colony, describing the rights he was giving them and the laws he expected them to obey in return. He said, "You shall be governed by laws of your own making and live a free, and if you will, a sober and industrious life. I shall not usurp the right of any, or oppress his person."[11]

Within ten years Penn gave the colonists more rights. In 1683 the assembly approved a second Frame of Government, which diminished the power held by wealthy landowners and gave the people more control over the government. Eight years later, in 1701, Penn wrote a new law called the Charter of Privileges, which granted people even more rights to govern themselves and stated that the legislature would be the only lawmaking body. Penn's Charter of Privileges was the first document of its kind to permit changes in the law through amendments, an idea that was later written into state and national constitutions in the United States.

William Penn named the capital of Pennsylvania "Philadelphia," based on Greek words meaning "City of Brotherly Love." Penn wanted the city to become a major commercial port.

## Building a Colony

William Penn also actively planned the physical development of his colony and its capital city in ways he thought would promote growth and the quality of life. For one thing, Penn wanted the capital to be a major commercial port. In the fall of 1681 he asked some trusted advisers to visit the colony and identify a good site for the capital, which Penn called "Philadelphia," from Greek words that mean "City of Brotherly Love." He said this city must be near the Delaware River in a place where the water was deep enough for ships to dock yet high enough above water to remain dry.

When the advisers returned to England, Penn worked with them and a surveyor to make sure Philadelphia would be a healthful and attractive city. They devised an orderly grid pattern with streets crossing each other at right angles. Unlike the streets in London, these streets were broad so that buildings would not be too close together, something Penn hoped would reduce the spread of fires. Streets were numbered or named for trees or plants. Penn asked Philadelphians to build homes in the middle of their plots with "ground on each side for gardens or orchards or fields, that it may be a green country town, which will never be burnt and always wholesome." [12]

As for rural Pennsylvania, Penn believed farmers should own enough land to prosper and that they should build their farms in ways that enhanced community life and helpfulness among neighbors. William Penn envisioned rural hamlets with the land divided into townships of around five thousand acres to be inhabited by about ten families. He suggested dividing the land into parcels shaped like pie slices, with homes near the tips so families would live fairly close to each other and to their church, shops, and other community buildings; however, farmers often found it more convenient to build homes closer to the middle of their parcel so they could reach their crops more easily.

Penn did not see the colony for himself until October 1682, when he arrived in Philadelphia aboard the ship *Welcome* along with one hundred settlers. He was heartened to see a town taking shape in the wilderness. The English settlers who had preceded him had built ten homes, a trading post–tavern, and a windmill, and they had planted gardens. More than a thousand settlers, along with Indians in canoes,

The treaties that William Penn made with the Native Americans between 1682 and 1684 were designed to ensure a harmonious and respectful relationship between settlers and Indians.

greeted Penn's group at the waterfront. They gave Penn a piece of soil with a twig embedded in it as a symbol of the land he governed.

## Relations with Indians

Shortly after he arrived, William Penn began meeting with local Native Americans, whom he approached in a spirit of goodwill and respect, in keeping with his religious beliefs. Harmonious relations with Indians were also vital for the peaceful colony he envisioned. In a meeting with Indian leaders, Penn said, "I will consider you as the same flesh and blood with the Christians, and the same as if one man's body were to be divided into two parts." [13] Penn earned their respect by walking among them unarmed and unguarded and by learning to speak their language. The Indians also admired Penn's physical stamina. As a boy, Penn had enjoyed racing and could still run and walk long distances.

Between 1682 and 1684 Penn made treaties with Native Americans. The language in one treaty with the Leni-Lenape, dated July 15, 1682, says, "The Great Spirit who made me and you, who rules the heavens and the Earth, and who knows the innermost thoughts of men, knows that I and my friends have a hearty desire to live in peace and friendship with you." [14] This treaty states that the settlers would pay the Indians for their land, that disputes between Indians and whites were to be arbitrated fairly, and that Indians accused of a crime were entitled to a trial by a jury including Indians and whites.

Penn's approach to Indian-white relations bore fruit. The Indians did not attack the settlers and even regarded them as an asset whose presence helped deter attacks from enemies to the north. Peaceful relations with Indians, along with Pennsylvania's other attractions, led to steady growth in the colony.

## A Prosperous Melting Pot

As Penn had hoped, his colony grew rapidly as he advertised it throughout Europe and newcomers wrote favorable reports urging others to come to Pennsylvania. Religious freedom, political rights, and economic opportunities were powerful incentives for many Europeans, and peace attracted many immigrants from war-torn southern Germany. Between 1682 and 1700 the population of Pennsylvania reached 20,000, and by 1750 it had reached 120,000.

By that time Philadelphia was the second-largest city in the colonies. Other towns were growing, too. Lancaster, founded in 1718, was home to about two thousand people, and York, Bethlehem, Carlisle, Reading, and Germantown were likewise thriving, with strong enterprises and institutions. Daniel Pastorius, the Mennonite founder of Germantown, said that his town had "its own court, its own burgomaster and council, together with the necessary officials, and well-regulated town laws, council regulations, and a town seal."[15] Some citizens worked in trades as linen weavers, tailors, shoemakers, locksmiths, or carpenters, and others were farmers.

Some settlers in Pennsylvania, such as this woodworker, earned a living by working in trades. Other tradespeople were weavers, tailors, shoemakers, locksmiths, carpenters, and farmers.

During the early years most colonists were Quakers from England, Wales, and Germany, but members of other persecuted religious sects soon arrived. The Protestant Reformation had spread throughout Europe after Martin Luther broke from Catholicism in his native Germany in the 1520s and founded Lutheranism. During the next century dozens of new Protestant religious groups formed and often found themselves in conflict with the majority in their homelands.

Those who found refuge in Pennsylvania included Baptists from northern European countries, Brethren (called Dunkers), Schwenkfelders (an Anabaptist sect), French Huguenots, and Moravians. Amish and Mennonites, two small religious pacifist sects from Germany, built farms in southeastern Pennsylvania. People began to call them "Pennsylvania Dutch" because they spoke German (*Deutsch* in German—a word English-speaking settlers heard as *Dutch*). Amish communities reflected their distinctive religious beliefs, as did Germantown, founded by Mennonites, and Bethlehem, founded by Moravians.

Jews, another group that had been persecuted throughout Europe, also came. Isaac Miranda, a native of Tuscany (now Italy), may have been the first Jew to live in Pennsylvania. Around 1715 Miranda moved to Lancaster and built a farm and trading post. During the 1730s Englishman Joseph Simon settled in Lancaster, where a Jewish community developed. Simon, a shop owner and trader, opened his

# America's First Paper Mill

William Penn advertised his colony heavily throughout Europe and was eager to attract skilled European craftspeople. After seeing one of Penn's ads, German-born William Rittenhouse came to Philadelphia in 1688. With financial help from Penn's land agent and two investors, Rittenhouse built America's first paper mill, which he operated with his son Timothy. The Rittenhouse mill was located near Monoshone Creek northwest of Philadelphia, close to sources of waterpower and a German-speaking population that included weavers known for making quality fabric. Rittenhouse used fabric scraps at the mill, where a giant-size trip hammer pounded them into the pulp that was made into paper.

After a flood destroyed the factory in 1700, colonists and other people in the region offered money and other help to keep it operating. The Rittenhouses built a stronger new mill near the same site.

home for religious services. A larger Jewish community grew in Philadelphia.

Along with religious freedom, the chance to own land attracted many settlers. As tenant farmers in Europe, they had rented someone else's land, and landowners controlled many aspects of their lives. Writing to friends back in Germany, settler Christopher Maur said, "Because one may hold as much property as one wishes, also pay for it when one desires, everybody hurries to take up some property." [16] New German, Dutch, and Swiss immigrants settled primarily in the fertile valleys west of the earliest settlements, where most became farmers, or they moved farther west, where the land was cheaper.

The chance for economic advancement also brought Scots-Irish settlers—Scots who had been living in Northern Ireland—to the colony. Many of them became traders and fur trappers in the rugged areas beyond the Allegheny Mountains. They appreciated the chance to trap and hunt without asking a landowner for permission and the opportunity to freely practice their Presbyterian religion.

By the 1750s hundreds of different religions were represented in the colony. The law permitted them all, and despite some conflicts, colonists developed tolerance and avoided the religious wars that had plagued Europe. As a result, the colony developed a cosmopolitan atmosphere and new ideas flourished. Although William Penn did not grow wealthy from his colony, he did reach his goals of providing a religious haven and of fostering economic growth.

Chapter Three

# Life in the Pennsylvania Colony

With its natural resources and its skillful, hardworking people, Pennsylvania developed a broad economy based on industry, agriculture, and trade. After 1720 Pennsylvania became the leader in the iron industry, and until about 1780 its farmers produced so much wheat that it was called "the Breadbasket of America." Philadelphia was a major commercial port and had become the political center of the colonies. Known as "the Athens of America" because of its cultural attractions, the city drew skilled tradespeople and craftsmen as well as professionals, including doctors, teachers, clergy, and lawyers, who wanted to live and work there.

A strong economy and the chance to succeed through one's own efforts meant that the average Pennsylvanian enjoyed a higher standard of living than the average European. Although most people worked hard for a living, prosperity gave some colonists time for leisure, literary and artistic pursuits, and activities that improved their communities.

## City Life

Because Philadelphia was a major port, each year hundreds of ships arrived there with dry goods, metal objects, and other items, such as sugar, molasses, rum, indigo, and mahogany from the West Indies. Ships left carrying meat, grain, flour, lumber, hemp, and tobacco.

Inside the city itself, fine brick buildings, made from the red clay that lined the riverbanks, distinguished Philadelphia from other colonial towns. As early as 1692 Robert Turner, a wealthy Irish merchant who built the city's first brick house, wrote in a letter to William Penn, "Some that built wooden Houses, are sorry for it; Brick Building is said to be as cheap. Brick are exceeding good." [17] Both public buildings and homes were often made of brick.

Wealthy citizens built spacious homes with elegant wood furnishings, glass windows, and whitewashed walls. Polished cabinets displayed fine china and silver bowls, plates, and cutlery, and silver or brass candlesticks adorned mantels and tables. Before 1750 people rarely used carpets; instead, they covered their wood floors with white sand arranged in swirling patterns. Each day servants cleared away the old sand, scrubbed the floors, and put down clean sand.

After becoming a major commercial port, Philadelphia was known as "the Athens of America." Pictured are brick buildings on High Street; brick was a common building material at this time.

Many household goods were imported, but some were made in the city itself. Shops displayed furniture, clocks, candles, metal goods, linens, and glassware as well as carriages, books, and clothing. Philadelphia's spacious marketplace held thirteen hundred feet of covered stalls offering an assortment of foods, including produce and meats from nearby farms. They also sold beverages, including wines, brandies, beer, and apple cider.

By the 1750s Philadelphians plied many trades, often related to the import-export and shipbuilding industries, or they provided goods and services. People could be seen loading and unloading cargo and keeping taverns and inns. There were wheelwrights, mechanics, barbers, printers, cabinetmakers, jewelers, metalworkers (working with pewter, silver, gold, brass, and tin), leather workers, weavers, locksmiths, shoemakers, coopers, and tailors. Women were more likely to work as ribbon weavers, lace weavers, button makers, milliners, and dressmakers. Stores did a lively business as Philadelphians and people visiting from rural areas bought various household goods and clothing.

Letters written in 1700 by William Penn's wife, Hannah, show that homemakers bought a variety of goods. She wrote about her need for "two pair of pewter candlesticks, some great candles . . . also some green

In eighteenth-century Philadelphia, women worked as weavers as well as button makers, milliners, and dressmakers.

ones . . . [a large] pewter basin, and . . . a new earthen one to wash in, also one of the stands to hold it . . . good butter; also cheese and candles."[18] Her list also included oil for her husband's sore leg, blue cloth to make shirts for the servants, and Madeira wine.

People's clothing and accessories revealed their class and sometimes their religion. Wealthy colonists could afford garments made of silk, satin, velvet, and fine wool, often in bright shades of blue, red, and gold. A typical well-to-do man wore a jacket and knee-length trousers in contrasting colors, silk stockings, and shoes with large silver buckles. Silver or gold ornaments and feather plumes adorned three-cornered hats of red, purple, blue, or other bright hues. Women wore gowns with a petticoat resembling a skirt, triangular-shaped shawls, and either a hat tied under the chin or a scarf. Children wore simple shifts until they were about six or seven. Then, boys wore breeches, woolen socks, shirts, and a vest for special occasions, with a leather or felt hat, and girls wore clothing similar to that of their mothers.

As in Europe, some men and women wore wigs made from either horsehair or human hair in black, brown, or coated with white powder. Wigmakers formed waves, curls, and rolls and added a braid down the back of men's wigs.

Quakers, regardless of economic class, dressed simply. Men wore black, brown, or gray, although some added colorful sashes and silver shoe buckles. Women also wore plain, muted clothing with simple bonnets, occasionally adding a red, blue, or green apron. Both genders avoided wigs and ornate hats.

Likewise, people of different classes ate differently, according to their means. A dinner at a Philadelphia mansion might feature several courses, with various meats and poultry—ham, beef, roast mutton, veal, chicken, pheasant, turkey—accompanied by potatoes, turnips, green peas or beans, and fruit pies, cheese, bread, and butter. Less affluent colonists ate simpler meals consisting of bread, cornmeal dishes, and less expensive meats, poultry, or fish.

Wealthier Philadelphians were often Quaker merchants, and their religion endorsed social service and good works. Along with altruistic non-Quakers, they found ways to help the less fortunate and improve the community, striving to make it a place of brotherly love.

In 1751, Benjamin Franklin, shown at left, established Pennsylvania Hospital, the first general hospital in America.

## Innovative Services

During the eighteenth century creative colonists improved the quality of life in Philadelphia, a place that became known for its civic spirit. The Quakers had already organized benevolent societies for needy people who were unable to work. Penn had also decreed that jails would aim to rehabilitate prisoners and teach them trades so they could earn an honest living.

Benjamin Franklin (1706–1790), a candlemaker's son who had left Boston for Philadelphia at age seventeen, contributed much to his new hometown. In 1736 Franklin urged Philadelphians to start a volunteer fire department, the first in the colonies, as well as a police force. At his initiative, Philadelphia's streets were paved beginning in the 1740s. Franklin also started the first general hospital in the country, Pennsylvania Hospital, in 1751, the same year he sparked a movement to install lamps powered by whale oil on major city streets.

A book lover who had mostly educated himself, Franklin established America's first lending library. Members paid fees that were used to buy books—scarce and expensive in those days—that they could then borrow. The idea of lending libraries spread throughout Pennsylvania and other colonies. Franklin also formed the Junto club for men who wanted to improve themselves and their communities by discussing literature, politics, history, poetry, and science. As other Junto groups were formed, they also carried out service projects.

# Slavery in the Colony

*Some Pennsylvanians could not choose their way of life. Slaves arrived as early as 1684; by 1730 they numbered about four thousand. Despite the apparent contradiction with their religious principles, some Quakers, including William Penn, owned slaves, most of whom worked as household servants.*

*Some colonists worked to ban slavery, but change came slowly. In 1688 Mennonites in Germantown signed a resolution against slavery, the first formal antislavery resolution in America. By the 1690s Quaker leaders discussed penalizing members who imported slaves. Quaker leaders in Philadelphia banned slaveholders from business meetings in 1758. Calling slavery un-Christian, they urged others to free their slaves. Quaker leader John Woolman discussed its evils, both in public and in his journal, which was later published as* The Journal and Essays of John Woolman:

> In procuring slaves on the Coast of Africa, many Children are stolen privately; Wars also are encouraged amongst the Negroes. . . . Many Groans arise from dying Men, which we hear not. Many Cries are uttered by Widows and Fatherless Children, which reach not our ears. . . . Cruel Tyranny is encouraged. The Hands of Robbers are strengthened, and thousands reduced to the most abject Slavery, who never injured us.

*Anthony Benezet also worked fervently to abolish slavery. By day he taught in a Quaker school; at night he educated slaves and free blacks. Benezet wrote antislavery pamphlets and helped found an abolition society.*

*As a result of these efforts, slave traders were banned from the Society of Friends in 1761, and slave ownership was outlawed a few years later.*

## Rural Life

Outside the cities, Pennsylvania's farmers worked hard to support their families and to supply food for their fellow colonists. During the 1700s the average farm in southeastern Pennsylvania was around 100 to 125 acres. Some of that land was left uncleared or was occupied by homes and farm buildings. About one-fifth was planted with grain, which was made into flour and used to feed livestock. Flax, vegetables, and fruits were grown on another 8 or 9 acres, while 13 to 15 acres of meadowland were left for cattle grazing. A small number of farms had small tobacco patches. Although some farmers could raise enough crops to sell some for cash, others, especially those in western Pennsylvania, often raised just enough for their own needs.

Most pioneers built simple log cabins with stone fireplaces when they arrived on the frontier. Later, if they owned livestock, they built wooden or stone barns. Because glass was imported and expensive, people substituted oiled paper, thinly sliced horn, or simply covered their window openings with wooden shutters. Candles, torches made from wood, or fish-oil lamps provided light, but most people retired at sunset.

Rural cabins were furnished simply with logs or plain wood furniture. Simple shelves held preserved foods, utensils, and cooking equipment, such as pots, iron kettles, a coffee pot, and a frying pan. Clothing was hung on wooden pegs, and a spinning wheel, used to make clothing, usually stood in a corner. Mattresses were made from feathers or were stuffed with straw.

Farm families worked hard to raise their own food and to make other things they needed. Although some communities had a blacksmith, cooper, wheelwright, carpenter, and a general store selling salt, coffee, tea, spices, cloth, buttons, tools, and certain other items, people provided for most of their own needs. Families usually owned a cow and one or more hogs, and the men caught fish in the streams and hunted wild deer, elks, bears, rabbits, pigeons, and turkeys. They raised corn, wheat, rye, peas, and potatoes. Some settlers had peach trees and, later, apple trees, and they gathered berries and herbs.

Men worked together on large jobs, such as clearing land and building barns and homes. Barn raisings combined a chore with a social event. When the work was finished, the men headed for the dinner table, where women had set out large platters of sausage, sauerkraut, and potatoes, along with soup, bread, butter, jams, jellies, apple butter, pies, and cakes.

Women prepared meals and made bread, butter and cheese, preserves, cider, and sausages. Meals varied by the season, although corn was a staple year-round. It was eaten fresh at harvest time, and during other months dried corn and cornmeal were used to make mush (cereal) and other dishes. Breakfast might be milk, coffee, bread, and johnnycake, a hotcake made from cornmeal. At midday people ate fresh fish or game in season or cured meats, such as bacon or ham, with corn, dumplings, and berries or preserves. Besides milk, people drank whiskey made from grains, spices, and sweeteners.

Country colonists wore simple clothing, usually homemade but sometimes store-bought. Deerskin was used for men's pants, shirts, vests, and for men's and women's jackets. During the summer, instead of the knee-length stockings they used in cooler months, men wore thin pants down to their feet. People of all ages wore home-tanned leather moccasins or shoes. Flax and wool were used to make fabric, either alone or combined to make linsey-woolsey. Linen cloth made from flax fibers was used for dresses, shirts, skirts, petticoats, aprons, bedsheets, and tablecloths. Wool making began in the spring, when sheep were sheared. Women cleaned the fleece carefully, then washed and dried it. They carded the wool, spun it into thread, and then either wove the thread into cloth on their own loom or hired a professional weaver.

Cloth was dyed with plant materials: Black walnut hulls yielded brown, and butternut bark made a muted yellow. Red dye came from the cochineal bug or madder roots. Blue dye was extracted from woad and indigo plants, and the Osage orange plant provided green dye.

In addition to cooking and making clothing, women reared children and made soap and other household supplies. All year they saved beef fat, called tallow, which was melted for

Many household supplies, such as soap, had to be made by hand. This duty often fell upon the women of the colony.

candlemaking. Bayberries, also called candleberries, were sometimes added for fragrance. Just as men worked in groups to complete large tasks such as clearing stumps, women gathered for quilting bees, sewing bees, and other jobs. They adorned their clothing and household goods with embroidery, fringes, lace, quilting, and other fancywork.

Indentured servants provided some help for farm families. In exchange for passage to America, these servants, called redemptioners, worked a certain number of years for the person who paid their fare to the shipping company. Under Pennsylvania law, former servants received clothing, about fifty acres of land, and sometimes money once their servitude ended. Many of them became successful businesspeople, tradespeople, and farmers.

## Education in the Colony

Access to education was another way Pennsylvanians could rise economically and take a more active role in civic life. The constitution adopted in 1682 declared that all children should learn to read and write by age twelve and that everyone should grow up learning a useful trade. Church groups founded most of the early schools in the colony in order to help children learn to read and understand the Bible and master basic writing and arithmetic skills. Quakers in Philadelphia founded the Friends' public school in 1689 for children whose parents could not afford to pay for a private education, and Presbyterian ministers founded many schools in Scottish settlements.

During the 1700s churches and concerned citizens organized more schools for the poor, and wealthy parents continued to hire tutors to teach their children. Children from more affluent families studied Latin, Greek, mathematics, literature, science, and history, and the young men often went on to college in Europe or New England.

Rural colonists had fewer educational opportunities, so parents who could read taught their own children, using whatever books they owned—usually a Bible and one or more almanacs. People in these communities sometimes pooled their money to hire a teacher, who boarded with a local family and taught in a one-room school.

To provide higher education, Benjamin Franklin and other prominent Philadelphians founded an academy at a school that had begun operating in 1740. In 1755 it became Pennsylvania's first

In 1682, Pennsylvania adopted a constitution that required children to learn to read and write by age twelve.

college—the College and Academy of Philadelphia, and ten years later it opened the first medical school in North America. It developed into a private institution, the University of Pennsylvania.

The university and other facilities and attractions helped to make Philadelphia a cultural center and popular place to visit. As transportation improved, more colonists had access to the capital city and other parts of Pennsylvania.

## Getting from Place to Place

Transportation was important in Pennsylvania because farmers needed to reach mills, markets, and trading posts, and merchants had to ship their goods. Early colonists traveled over the same paths the Indians had made, and as villages and towns developed, people widened these paths so they could take cartloads of goods from place to place. They used log rafts, dugout canoes, or rowboats to cross streams. By the 1700s people

Many bridges had been built by the 1700s to assist transportation, including this one over Front Street in Philadelphia.

had built bridges, strong enough to carry a wagon, over some streams. Ferries along the Delaware River helped people travel within Pennsylvania and also to make connections to New York, New England, and other destinations.

Certain towns, including Lancaster, York, Carlisle, Allentown, Bethlehem, and Easton, developed along the routes farmers took to reach sawmills, gristmills, and markets. In the early 1700s a heavy wagon could not cover more than thirty miles in a day, so travelers made stops in towns like these. The colonists also built a network of roads to Philadelphia and other key cities.

In 1700 the government of Pennsylvania instructed the leaders of its counties to set up divisions called townships. Each township was told to choose a supervisor, whose jobs included building and maintaining roads. However, local officials sometimes ignored the condition of the roads and many were poorly maintained.

Several major roads were completed, such as Queen's Road, connecting Chester with Philadelphia, in 1706. Old York Road, linking Philadelphia with New York City, was finished a few years later. Conestoga Road, connecting people in the Susquehanna Valley with Philadelphia, received heavy traffic from wagons and stagecoaches, and

# A Practical New Wagon

In order to carry large loads long distances over varied terrain, Pennsylvanians developed a new kind of wagon. It may have originated with German farmers in the early 1700s, but the Dutch also developed wagons with similar features. It was called the Conestoga wagon, after the Conestoga Valley in Lancaster County.

With their white canvas tops, red upper bodies, and Prussian blue bottoms, these wagons, which cost about $250 in the 1750s, were both colorful and sturdy. The deep body was slanted like a boat so that the contents moved toward the middle when the wagon went up or down hills. The six-inch-thick wheels were high, which enabled the wagon to cross streams. Arches built across the body held a canvas top to protect contents from the rain, so people began calling them covered wagons.

Fully loaded, the wagons weighed two to three thousand pounds and required six to eight horses. Drivers sat on the left side in order to control the left wheel horse—the start of the American custom of driving on the right side of the road.

By the late 1750s hundreds of farmers were using Conestogas to transport grain and other produce to market. After the Revolutionary War, these wagons became the major mode for transporting goods to the Ohio Valley. Thousands of pioneers later crossed the continent in a version of the covered wagon called a prairie schooner. By the 1850s, however, canal and rail transportation had replaced the wagon.

Pioneers often traveled west in Conestoga wagons, developed by Pennsylvanians in the 1700s.

wheels tore up the dirt and created deep grooves, which turned to mud when it rained. By 1776 stagecoach lines connected south-central Pennsylvania with Philadelphia. These improvements helped people to reach the port city more easily and improved trade.

Other colonial ports were growing, too. As Baltimore became increasingly important, leaders in Pennsylvania feared that the rival port would gain more business if they did not improve transportation. In 1792 Philadelphians paid a private company to begin building the Lancaster Turnpike, a hard-surfaced stone road. Completed in 1795, it stretched from Lancaster to Philadelphia and could accommodate wagons twice as heavy as those that traveled on the old dirt roads.

Water transportation also improved through the years. The first artificial waterway was constructed in 1797, when the Conewago Canal was built on the west bank of the Susquehanna below York Haven. It allowed boats to bypass the Conewago Falls and linked Columbia with a turnpike that ran to Philadelphia.

## Social Life

Pennsylvanians did not spend all of their time working, trading, or taking goods to market. They enjoyed socializing and saw their fellow colonists when they attended church or weddings and funerals, as well as during recreational activities. Talking—at home or in taverns—was one of the most common pastimes in cities and rural areas. Men gathered to discuss business, politics, and other topics or to play cards or billiards. Bowling was another popular pastime, and horse racing, bullbaiting, and cockfighting were favorite spectator sports. Women enjoyed visiting with friends, too, and met at tea parties and sewing circles. City residents could visit art galleries, traveling acts or exhibits, theatrical productions, and lectures.

Although many Quaker settlers frowned on theaters, dancing, and musical entertainment, other colonists enjoyed these activities, just as they had in Europe. New dances from France and England became popular among wealthier urban colonists, and some young people took dancing lessons. Traveling dance and music teachers offered lessons outside the cities, where rural colonists also taught their children traditional folk dances from their homelands.

Young people usually played simple games that did not require much equipment, including tag, hopscotch, leapfrog, sack races, and blindman's buff. Other favorites were marbles and ninepins, which resembles bowling. In the roll-the-hoop game, players raced toward a finish line while rolling a big wooden hoop. Many girls enjoyed dolls, either store-bought European dolls with china heads and elegant wardrobes or homemade cloth or cornhusk varieties. Spinning tops and whirligigs were popular with both boys and girls.

This boy is holding spinning tops, a toy popular with Pennsylvania children.

Summer sports included swimming and fishing. In the country, boys wrestled, ran races, and practiced shooting or throwing knives at a target. During the winter, children enjoyed sledding, ice skating, and sleighing. Alexander Graydon, who grew up in the colony, later described good times on the Delaware and Schuylkill Rivers: "The exercises of swimming and skating were so much within the reach of the boys of Philadelphia, that it would have been surprising, had they neglected them or even had they not excelled in them." He called Philadelphians "the best and most elegant skaters in the world."[19]

Although rural colonists had little spare time, they managed to combine work and pleasure at their barn raisings, stump pullings, apple parings, corn huskings, and other work-play gatherings, often followed by music, dancing, and refreshments. The autumn butchering of hogs and cattle in German communities was a festive occasion. One observer described this event: "The day was spent cutting up the meat, making sausage, rendering the lard, making scrapple, and smoking the hams and bacons over fires of green hickory chips. . . . At night after partaking of schnatz betz (rye whiskey) all go home carrying with them as much sausage and fresh meat as needed."[20]

Events like these helped people get their work done and also build a sense of neighborliness and community. As they lived, worked, and socialized in their new homeland, Pennsylvanians built on their ancestral traditions and developed a new sense of themselves as Americans.

## Chapter Four

# Revolutionary Years

During the 1700s Pennsylvania became embroiled in wars between England and France and their respective Indian allies and then in the American Revolution. These wars divided Pennsylvanians, often along religious, economic, and regional lines. As conflicts with Great Britain escalated, Pennsylvanians disagreed about what course the colony should pursue. Whereas some people wanted to break away from the British, others favored various compromises. Still others wanted to remain a part of Britain. Pacifists were often at odds with both sides as they tried to stay neutral and avoid war-related activities. Historian John C. Miller describes the situation this way: "Here the division [over how to deal with Britain] arose from differences based on religion, sectionalism, nationality, and Indian policy—most of the major causes of political action in colonial America."[21]

Mounting British interference increased revolutionary fervor and brought major political changes in Pennsylvania. By the 1770s most people wanted independence, even if it meant war, but most of the assembly disagreed. Revolutionary leaders finally prevailed over the conservative assembly, and a new legislature committed to independence was formed. Pennsylvanians joined the fight as soldiers, political leaders, diplomats, and as civilians providing supplies for the army and making sacrifices on the home front. They played a key role in freeing their country from European rule.

## Disputes over Military Action

Between 1689 and 1748 England and France fought three wars over lands in North America. Whereas France claimed Canada and the Mississippi basin, Britain controlled the thirteen colonies along the Atlantic Coast, and both sides wanted the lands held by the other. Their disputes remained unsettled, and more armed confrontations occurred during the 1750s, some of them in Pennsylvania.

Many colonists criticized the assembly for refusing to build and supply a militia or fortify the frontier. The Quaker-dominated assembly had also refused to send money for guns and ammunition when New England leaders requested help from other colonies during King George's War (1744–1748). During that war England and its colonial allies fought against the French. The assembly did vote to send food in the form of "wheat and other grain"[22] to New England. Governor George Thomas, who did not belong to a pacifist religious group, decided to send "grains" of gunpowder.

Disagreements over military action intensified during the French and Indian Wars (1754–1763), when France again challenged Britain's domination of North America. By 1750 Indian–white relations had deteriorated in Pennsylvania. The proprietors who succeeded William Penn did not honor the treaties he had made and increasing numbers of white settlers moved onto Native American lands, forcing the Indians farther west. As a result, most Indians sided with the French during the war, and both sides attacked frontier settlements in Pennsylvania and other colonies.

Western Pennsylvanians became angry when the assembly refused to send troops or build more forts to protect them. Unlike other colonies, Pennsylvania also did not pass laws requiring able-bodied men to serve in the military until 1755, and pacifists could be excused from the military on religious grounds. To protect themselves, some frontiersmen banded together to attack Indians, which led to more Indian–white conflicts and disagreements between frontier families and the assembly. These kinds of disputes were unresolved when the French and Indian Wars ended.

During the French and Indian Wars, some frontiersmen banded together to attack Indians.

## Uniting Against Britain

New problems soon developed with Great Britain, which had accumulated large debts during the French and Indian Wars. Its expenses increased when it sent thousands of troops to defend the colonies against possible future attacks from France. Since the colonies were prospering, the British decided to tax them on the purchase of imported goods to help pay for the war effort.

Since British laws also forbid the colonists from making numerous goods themselves, they were forced to pay taxes if they wanted these items. Laws that banned Americans from producing cloth and other items angered people in Pennsylvania. By the late 1700s they had the raw materials and other resources they needed to operate factories and to make these goods themselves and did not think Britain had the right

In 1755 during the French and Indian Wars, British soldiers help the colonists defend themselves against the French and the Indians.

to stop them. Defying the British, Philadelphian Benjamin Rush organized a group of Pennsylvanians to begin making cloth on a large scale so colonists would not have to buy British goods at unfairly high prices or lack clothing if the British refused to sell it to them.

Pennsylvanians protested along with other colonists who opposed being taxed without their consent or any representation in Parliament (Britain's lawmaking body). In his famous *Letters from a Farmer in Pennsylvania, to the Inhabitants of the British Colonies,* assemblyman John Dickinson wrote, "If Great-Britain can order us to come to her for necessaries we want, and can order us to pay what taxes she pleases before we take them away, or when we land them here, we are as abject slaves as France and Poland can shew in wooden shoes, and with uncombed hair."[23]

Colonists came together to publicly oppose the Stamp Act, another British tax, which required them to buy special stamps for newspapers and legal documents. They celebrated when Britain repealed the tax in 1766. After Britain began taxing tea in 1769, Pennsylvanians boycotted British tea, wine, cloth, furniture, china, silver, and jewelry. Angry Philadelphians demonstrated at the docks when tea-laden ships arrived, and they later passed a law stating that anyone who helped receive, sell, or even unload British tea would be considered an enemy of his country—meaning America, not their countries of origin in Europe.

By that time about 40 percent of the American colonists were of non-British ancestry, with no ties to Britain. In diverse Pennsylvania, a large number of colonists had come from Germany and other countries. Furthermore, many colonists of British descent felt no loyalty to Britain, either. Instead, they felt like Americans, part of a new nation they had formed themselves, and they resented British rule.

Outside Pennsylvania, thousands of people shared those attitudes. More and more Pennsylvanians thought the thirteen colonies should unite to deal with Britain. They moved closer together in 1774 after the British closed Boston's port to punish colonists for the Boston Tea Party, in which Patriots (colonists opposing the British) boarded British ships and dumped tea into the harbor to protest the tea taxes. Philadelphians

Angry about remaining subject to Great Britain's laws and unfair taxes, colonists protest by dumping British tea shipments into Boston Harbor.

made speeches supporting colonists in Boston. A large group of Philadelphians met to pass the Pennsylvania Resolutions on the Boston Port Act, which called the British action "unconstitutional, oppressive to the inhabitants of that town, dangerous to the liberties of the British colonies." The resolutions mandated a committee of Philadelphians to correspond with leaders in other colonies and to organize "a congress of deputies" that would seek ways of "procuring relief for our suffering brethren, obtaining redress of American grievances, securing our rights and liberties, and re-establishing peace and harmony between Great Britain and these colonies, on a constitutional foundation."[24]

Leaders from all thirteen colonies agreed to send representatives to a meeting in Philadelphia to discuss their problems with Britain. On September 5, 1774, fifty-six men from every colony but Georgia (which agreed to follow the group's decisions) gathered for the First Continental Congress. One representative, the speaker of the Pennsylvania assembly, was Joseph Galloway, a conservative who favored unity with Britain. He submitted a plan for reconciling Britain and the colonies under a new imperial constitution, but it was rejected. Philadelphia merchant Thomas Mifflin was among those who opposed Galloway's plan and called for firm limits on British rule as well as a formal boycott of British goods. The congress finally approved a declaration stating that the colonists had certain rights, including life, liberty, trial by jury, and representation in the British Parliament.

The Second Continental Congress in Philadelphia produced the Olive Branch Petition (the last page shown here), asking King George III to restore peaceful relations with the colonies.

When the Second Continental Congress met in May in Philadelphia's State House, Pennsylvanian John Dickinson presented his Olive Branch Petition, which asked Great Britain to restore peaceful relations with the colonies. Richard Penn, a descendant of William Penn, agreed to present the petition to the Crown, but King George refused to read it, saying that he would deal with the colonies individually, not as a united group.

On April 18, 1775, fighting broke out between British soldiers and colonial militiamen at Lexington and Concord in Massachusetts after the British moved to seize guns and gunpowder the colonists had stored in those towns. A group of Pennsylvania patriots responded to this battle by writing a resolution urging their fellow colonists to form militias and arm themselves, saying, "All persons here present will associate together to defend with arms their property, liberty and lives, against the attempts to deprive them of it."[25]

After the confrontations at Lexington and Concord, the Continental Congress, which was still meeting in Philadelphia, began organizing a colonial army and making other preparations for war.

## Taking Sides

Many Pennsylvanians still opposed a war against Britain, even though some of them supported American independence. Opponents of war included religious pacifists as well as wealthy landowners and merchants who conducted business with Britain. Some of these people also did not want the colonies to become a separate nation. Some Quakers and Anglicans joined forces in an effort to have King George declare Pennsylvania a royal colony directly under the authority of the Crown instead of William Penn's descendants, who had left the Quaker faith and were no longer pacifists. Other Quakers and Anglicans took a neutral or moderate position, as did many German Americans.

Pro-British groups increasingly found themselves in the minority as more colonists supported independence. Most of the Scots-Irish settlers living in western Pennsylvania and their Presbyterian allies in Philadelphia were committed to that cause, as were most inland farmers and Baptists, but people from various walks of life could be found on both sides. Patriotic colonists spoke eloquently about their ideals. One Pennsylvania woman, whose brother had joined a colonial militia, wrote,

> I know this, that as free I can die but once, but as a slave, I shall
> not be worthy of life.... These are the sentiments of all my sister
> Americans. They have sacrificed both assemblies, parties of
> pleasure, tea drinking and finery to that great spirit of

Thomas Paine published a pamphlet called *Common Sense* in which he argued in favor of American separation from Britain.

patriotism that actuates all ranks and degrees of people throughout this extensive continent. [26]

The Pennsylvania assembly was still dominated by conservatives who sought a nonviolent resolution to British-American problems. In November 1775 it instructed Pennsylvania's representatives to the Continental Congress to "exert your utmost endeavors to agree upon and recommend such measures as [will] afford the best prospect of obtaining redress of American grievances, and restoring the union and harmony between Great Britain and the colonies so essential to the welfare and happiness of both countries." [27]

However, popular opinion favored independence, especially after two Philadelphians produced a pamphlet that convinced more colonists that British rule was both impractical and intolerable. Benjamin Rush, a physician and patriot, urged newly arrived Englishman Thomas Paine to write down his articulate arguments favoring separation. Rush was so impressed with the essays that he had them published in a pamphlet, which he called *Common Sense*. Paine listed the ways Americans suffered from British control without gaining anything in return. He wrote, "We have it in our power to begin the world anew. . . . America shall make a stand, not for herself alone, but for the world." [28] *Common Sense* was read throughout the colonies, and Pennsylvanians discussed Paine's ideas with great interest.

When the Boston patriotic leader Samuel Adams visited Pennsylvania in 1776, he noticed more patriotism than he had observed the year before. Adams wrote, "The Martial [military] Spirit throughout this Province is astonishing, it arose all of a Sudden. . . . Quakers and all are carried away with it." [29] Most Quakers who supported independence advocated peaceful methods, however, not the use of force. Their leaders instructed them not to take sides, pay taxes for military purposes, or engage in any war-related business, or they might be voted out of the Society of Friends.

That spring and summer, British troops fought more battles against the small, ill-equipped colonial army led by General George Washington. Thousands more British soldiers arrived from England, and the British commander asked for an unconditional surrender. In Philadelphia, delegates at the Second Continental Congress agreed that a peaceful settlement was no longer possible and that they must now form a new government. They organized a navy and a postal service and asked a committee that included Benjamin Franklin to draft the new nation's Declaration of Independence, which would state that the colonies were now free of British rule. That June, they made plans to vote on the declaration, which had been written primarily by Thomas Jefferson of Virginia.

Nobody was certain whether the seven delegates from Pennsylvania would approve the declaration. Two of these men were absent on July 2, 1776, the day of the vote, but three of the remaining five—Franklin, John Morton, and James Wilson—voted "yes" with the majority; Charles Humphreys and Thomas Willing voted "no." The *Pennsylvania Evening Post* announced, "This day the Continental Congress declared

The Second Continental Congress adopted the Declaration of Independence from British rule on July 4, 1776.

the United Colonies Free and Independent States."[30] A few days later, on July 4, the congress adopted the declaration. Nine Pennsylvanians—the highest number from any colony—signed the document.

## A New Colonial Government

By 1776 many Pennsylvanians feared that the neutrals and British loyalists that still dominated the assembly would refuse to support a militia and the expanding fight against Britain. Citizens voiced this concern by sending numerous petitions supporting independence to the assembly.

Pennsylvanians became more vocal after the Continental Congress passed a resolution recommending that each colony form a government that would safeguard the general welfare. On May 20 about four thousand people gathered outside the State House in the rain to support a new colonial government and a new constitutional convention. With no support, the Pennsylvania assembly voted itself out of existence. The people of Pennsylvania had taken a step unique in the colonies by demanding a government that was committed to American independence.

In June, 108 delegates met to form a new government. They included many younger, middle-class men, as well as older patriots such as Benjamin Franklin. After agreeing to raise a militia of at least forty-five hundred men, these delegates told their fellow Pennsylvanians to begin selecting representatives for the new assembly and to choose men who were prepared to "secure liberty, property, and the sacred right of conscience."[31] These leaders also encouraged able-bodied men to join the army.

## Struggle for Freedom

Although the colonists had declared their independence, they faced a long, difficult struggle to achieve their goal. Pennsylvanians contributed in various ways on and off the battlefield, and daily life changed as men left to join the army and their families took on additional burdens to keep homes, farms, and businesses running in their absence.

Soldiers faced serious privations and were exposed to malnutrition and diseases as well as the threats on the battlefield. Fearful that these

Many soldiers suffered from malnutrition and disease while serving in the army.

difficulties would cause many recruits to desert the army, George Washington and other leaders encouraged Thomas Paine to continue writing to inspire people during the war. Paine, a soldier himself, wrote a series of pamphlets called *The Crisis* between 1776 and 1783. One famous passage urged people to stand firm in the face of adversity and not to be merely "sunshine patriots." Paine wrote,

> These are the times that try men's souls: The summer soldier and the sunshine patriot will, in this crisis, shrink from the service of his country; but he that stands it Now, deserves the love and thanks of man and woman. Tyranny, like hell, is not easily conquered; yet we have this consolation with us, that the harder the conflict the more glorious the triumph. [32]

Although most Quakers were pacifists, some formed a separate denomination that allowed its members to fight in the war against Britain.

Quakers and members of other peace sects (Amish, Mennonites, Moravians, and Brethren, or Dunkers) were forbidden to fight or engage in any military activity involving violence against other people. Although some local draft laws permitted people to pay a fee or to hire a substitute to avoid military service, Quakers also rejected that practice as unfair. Some Quakers performed humanitarian acts, such as nursing the wounded from either side. They also found other ways to contribute. When British officers occupied her home in Philadelphia, Quaker Lydia Darragh listened to their secret meetings and found a way to get the information she heard to the colonial army encamped at Whitemarsh.

Some members of pacifist sects did join the military, which meant expulsion from their religious community. One group of men led by Timothy Matlock formed a separate denomination called the Fighting (or Free) Quakers that permitted its members to fight. Other Quakers who joined the military were author Thomas Paine and political leader Thomas Mifflin, who had served in both the Pennsylvania assembly and the Continental Congress and would later be elected governor. He was among nearly a thousand Quakers who were denounced during the Revolution, usually for becoming soldiers.

Other Pennsylvanians supported the war effort by providing military supplies and food for the troops. As the iron-making center of early America, Pennsylvania contributed more armaments, including guns and ammunition, than any other colony. Paper from the Rittenhouse paper mill, one of the few in early America, was used to make gun wadding and cartridges for muskets. Grain and meat from Pennsylvania's farms were sent to military camps.

While soldiers fought on the battlefield, civilian Pennsylvanians faced dangers, too. Pacifists were sometimes attacked, and their homes were ransacked. In Philadelphia and throughout the Delaware Valley, soldiers from both sides punished Quakers, whom they accused of supporting the other side.

Residents of Philadelphia experienced fear and uncertainty as British and American troops fought over the city and alternately occupied it. Not only was Philadelphia a key port in a strategic location, but it was also the home to the Continental Congress, where colonists had declared their independence, and so both sides regarded it as a prize. During 1776, when British troops stationed in New York and New Jersey threatened Philadelphia, Congress moved to Baltimore. It returned in March 1777 after the British failed to seize the city. Later that fall, after defeating General Washington's troops at the Battle of Brandywine, the British again headed for Philadelphia, and Congress moved again, first to Lancaster, Pennsylvania, and then to York.

# A Philadelphian Gains Wartime Support

During the Revolutionary War Benjamin Franklin was asked to help his country once again, this time in the key role of international diplomat. Franklin was renowned in Europe as a writer, inventor, and philosopher as well as the scientist who had made important discoveries about electricity. His job was to obtain support, in the form of money and troops, from France.

In May 1776 King Louis XIV agreed to send $1 million in arms and munitions to the American cause, and Spain also pledged financial support. The French agreed to join the American war effort in February 1778, and their support played a key role in helping the colonial army defeat England.

In April 1782 Franklin represented the colonies at peace talks in Paris with Richard Oswald of Britain, then oversaw the signing of the Treaty of Paris, which officially ended the war in 1783.

From September 1777 until June 1778, British troops occupied Philadelphia and moved into people's homes, often without permission. Congress declared that any person who furnished supplies or military information to the British would be considered a traitor. American troops guarded the rivers leading into the city so British ships could not get through, and they set fire to the mills outside the city, which created food shortages for Americans as well as the British. The colony's leaders distributed rations of salted beef to Philadelphians who needed food.

Philadelphians waited anxiously on October 4, 1777, as British and American troops fought at nearby Germantown. Diarist Deborah Logan wrote,

> We could hear the firing, and knew of the engagement. . . . Toward evening many wagons full of the wounded arrived in the city, whose groans and sufferings were enough to move the most inhuman heart to pity. The American prisoners were carried to the State House lobbies, and had, of course, to wait until the British surgeons dressed their own men. But in a very short time the streets were filled with the women of the city, carrying up every kind of refreshment which they might be supposed to want, with lint and linen and lights in abundance for their accommodation. [33]

Although the British won that battle and held Philadelphia, the colonial army gained control of the surrounding region, and British troops could not hold the city for long. Under General Henry Clinton, they withdrew and marched toward New York. Once again, colonial troops entered Philadelphia, and the Continental Congress returned to the city, where it remained for the rest of the war.

Later in 1778 British troops were able to seize Philadelphia again for a brief time, despite a gallant effort from Washington's forces. Washington headed for Whitemarsh, then to Valley Forge, Pennsylvania, where his troops endured a dreadful winter before resuming the fight.

# Suffering at Valley Forge

*While the British enjoyed the hospitality of Tory families in Philadelphia, colonial troops spent a harsh winter at Valley Forge, located on a high plain about twenty-five miles west of Philadelphia. From there, Washington thought they could attack British troops heading into Philadelphia or escape into wilderness areas to the west in case of a British attack.*

*About eleven thousand soldiers representing every colony followed Washington into Valley Forge that December 19. They included African Americans and Native Americans and ranged in age from twelve to men in their fifties and sixties. The men built huts on the snow, with twelve men assigned to each one. They lacked enough food, clothing, blankets, and shoes, and the Continental Congress did not have the resources to help. More than three thousand men died; others suffered from frozen, bleeding feet; malnutrition; and diseases. They needed about 34,577 pounds of meat and 168 barrels of flour a day, and Washington asked farmers to send grain. To boost morale, Washington convinced Baron Friedrich von Steuben, a German officer, to teach them professional drills.*

*Surgeon Albigence Waldo described their plight in his diary, excerpts of which are available online.*

December 14: The Army, which has been surprisingly healthy hitherto, now begins to grow sickly from the continued fatigues they have suffered.... I am Sick—discontented and out of humour. Poor food—hard lodging—Cold Weather—fatigue—Nasty Cloaths—nasty Cookery—Vomit half my time.... Why are we sent here to starve and Freeze—What sweet Felicities have I left at home; A charming Wife—pretty Children—Good Beds—good Food—good Cookery.

## War's End

During the final years of the war, Philadelphia continued to be a center of both military conflicts and political activities. In March 1778 a British peace commission visited Philadelphia to negotiate with colonial leaders. It offered to meet all of the Americans' demands but not grant them independence. Congress rejected this offer, and the fighting continued.

The British surrender to French general Rochambeau following the Battle of Yorktown, October 19, 1781.

By then, however, the tide had turned in favor of the American troops. In September 1778 Washington and French general Jean-Baptiste-Donatien de Vimeur, comte de Rochambeau, took about sixty-five hundred combined troops to Philadelphia. From there, they planned the strategy that eventually enabled them to defeat British general Lord Charles Cornwallis's troops at the Battle of Yorktown, leading to the British surrender on October 19, 1781.

For several years colonial leaders had been preparing for independence and a new government. The Continental Congress had adopted the Articles of Confederation, which the Pennsylvania legislature approved on July 9, 1778. These articles united the colonies into one nation. At war's end, Philadelphia became the capital of that nation and the scene of major political developments, and Pennsylvania faced new challenges as a state rather than a colony.

## Chapter Five

# A Dynamic New State

T he second state to join the union, Pennsylvania continued to play a key role in the political, economic, and social development of the new United States. Its democratic traditions influenced the writing of the federal constitution, and with its Quaker roots, Pennsylvania became a leader in the fight against slavery.

The state's population kept growing, although some people left Pennsylvania after the war. Loyalists and pacifists had been harshly criticized, and some immigrated to Canada or England. By 1800 virtually all Native Americans were gone. Some groups had kept moving westward until they reached Ohio, where they formed new settlements, and the remaining Delaware moved to Canada or to government-designated reservations in the West.

Although Pennsylvania faced problems, including economic ones, after the Revolutionary War, the state benefited from its abundant natural resources and solid economy. The iron industry, and the discovery of coal and oil in the state, made Pennsylvania the industrial center of the nation. Transportation kept pace as new turnpikes were chartered to link Philadelphia with Trenton, New Jersey, and other cities. Industrial wealth helped the state support its growing population and fostered social and cultural growth as new towns and cities developed in the state's western frontier and eastern cities continued to thrive.

# Symbol of Freedom: The Liberty Bell

In 1751, to commemorate the fiftieth anniversary of the 1701 charter written by William Penn, the Pennsylvania assembly placed an order for a large bell with the Whitechapel Foundry in England. They planned to place the bell in the State House, where the assembly held its meetings. Inscribed on the side of the metal bell were the words, "Proclaim Liberty thro' all the Land to all the Inhabitants thereof," from a verse in the Book of Leviticus in the King James Bible. Isaac Norris, the speaker of the assembly, thought this was a suitable way to honor the liberties Pennsylvanians had enjoyed since the founding of the colony.

The bell arrived in 1752 but was not hung until March 1753. Norris noticed at once that it was cracked, so he had two local foundrymen recast it. The one-ton bell was then placed in the State House.

In July 1776 the Declaration of Independence was read in public places throughout Pennsylvania. Philadelphians crowded the State House yard to hear it on July 8, and the bell, which became known as the Liberty Bell, rang out, along with numerous church bells, as a symbol of freedom. Since then, the Liberty Bell has also been rung to celebrate various patriotic occasions, and the old State House has been renamed Independence Hall.

The Liberty Bell is a symbol of freedom for the United States.

Sometime between 1817 and 1846, the bell cracked again but historians do not know when or how this happened. Some people claimed that it cracked while it was being rung for a special occasion, for example George Washington's birthday in 1832 or the death of Chief Justice John Marshall in 1835, but these accounts cannot be confirmed.

## Postwar Challenges

After the Revolution, the new United States faced many economic and political problems, which Pennsylvania shared. Like other Revolutionary War veterans, many soldiers from Pennsylvania had not been paid for their military service. When the Continental Congress adopted the Articles of Confederation, the articles did not give Congress the authority to levy taxes or raise money in any other way that would provide revenues to the government. Congress did ask each state to help pay off the nation's war debts, including back pay the government owed its soldiers. Some states contributed, but others did not. None sent as much money as Congress had requested.

Philadelphia's State House is where Congress first met after the Revolution, and where the Liberty Bell was hung in March 1753.

Two years after the war, soldiers in Pennsylvania still had not been paid. Some of them had remained with their units instead of heading home because they could not afford to leave without their pay. In 1783 hundreds of Pennsylvania veterans marched from Lancaster to Philadelphia, where they demonstrated in front of Independence Hall, where Congress had its meetings, and demanded their money. John Dickinson, a prominent Philadelphia lawyer who had long been a member of Congress, tried to calm the crowd. The men grudgingly agreed to return to their base at Lancaster, where they waited for a resolution to their problem.

Congress worried that more soldiers would come to Philadelphia and some might even become violent. In June, it moved the capital to Princeton, New Jersey, where it remained until the new government devised a plan to pay the veterans in November 1783.

Pennsylvania faced other problems as the value of continental currency sank lower and lower. During the Revolution, Congress had issued paper money, much of it printed by the Philadelphia firm of Hall and Sellers, to finance the war, but this currency was backed with inadequate reserves of gold and silver. Congress had planned to redeem

At the Constitutional Convention of 1787, delegates from each of the thirteen colonies meet to establish the governmental structure that the United States would adopt.

the currency by having each colony levy taxes after the war, but this did not happen as planned. As a result, the currency was not worth much, and people joked that it might as well be used as wallpaper or to light a cigar.

During this time, many citizens could not afford to run their businesses or buy farming equipment, and some families struggled to obtain clothing, shoes, and other necessities. They petitioned the state and national government to help them with these problems and to devise a sound economic policy for the new nation.

## The Constitutional Convention

To address these economic problems and other issues facing the fledgling country, leaders met in Philadelphia in 1787. All thirteen colonies sent delegates to this national convention, where they discussed ways to develop a stronger central government and write the laws for the United States. Instead of merely amending the Articles of Confederation, Congress decided to reorganize the government.

Originally, these men had planned to give each state one vote in Congress, but states with large populations complained that that was unfair. In response, smaller states worried that larger states would have too much control over the others if they had more votes. A compromise was reached. Two branches of Congress were established—a Senate, where every state had two members, and a House of Representatives, based on the population in each state.

The group also decided that the United States would have a president and would aim to achieve a balance of power among three branches of government: executive, legislative, and judicial. Virginia delegate James Madison was assigned to put these ideas in writing, and this document became the Constitution of the United States. One of Pennsylvania's representatives, Gouverneur Morris, a New Yorker who had been living and working in Philadelphia, headed the committee that wrote the final draft of the Constitution.

After the Constitution was approved, it was signed, with eight men from Pennsylvania among the signers, the most from any of the new states. They included Benjamin Franklin, at age eighty-two the oldest delegate at the convention and a respected elder statesman. Another signer was Pennsylvania delegate James Wilson, who had influenced many of his colleagues by eloquently arguing for a strong national government that derived its power from the people, not from state government officials.

Delaware became the first state when it ratified the new Constitution on December 7; Pennsylvania became the second on December 12. By May 29, 1790, all thirteen colonies had ratified the Constitution and become states.

## The Nation's Capital

Philadelphia continued to serve as the capital of the United States and the place where Congress met after the war until the capital was moved, first to New York, then to Washington, D.C., in 1800. At the turn of the nineteenth century, Philadelphia remained prosperous as a major port and center of trade, and its citizens

Gouverneur Morris led the committee that wrote the final draft of the Constitution.

developed cultural and educational institutions that were admired throughout the nation. Educational facilities increased, and Philadelphians continued to publish influential books and newspapers.

Foreign visitors praised the appearance of both the city and its people. Swiss chocolate maker Philippe Suchard wrote,

> Most visitors to Philadelphia were taken by the charm of its broad, flagged streets. It is most bountifully provided with fresh water, which is showered and jerked about, and turned on and poured off, everywhere. The Waterworks, which are on a height near the city, are no less ornamental than useful, being tastefully laid out as a public garden, and kept in the best and neatest order. The river is dammed at this point and forced by its own power into certain high tanks or reservoirs, when the whole city, to the top stories of the houses, is supplied at a very trifling expense. [34]

A well-traveled Hungarian visitor said Philadelphia was "one of the most lovely" cities in the world. Commenting on its sixty-four public libraries and fifty newspapers and periodicals, he called it "the center of academic erudition and the cradle of science." [35]

Philadelphia suffered the effects of the devastating yellow fever epidemic that struck the United States in 1793. Other cities on the East Coast were also hard-hit by this mosquito-borne disease, which probably came into the country on ships from Santo Domingo. Philadelphia hospitals were among the best in the nation, and many victims from the region were brought there for treatment. About five thousand people, some 10 percent of the city's population, died that year. The epidemic finally ended when cold weather killed off the mosquitoes and their larvae that autumn.

Throughout the 1800s Philadelphia remained the largest city in the state, even after Harrisburg, located in southeast Pennsylvania on the Susquehanna River, became the state capital in 1812. In 1860 the population of Philadelphia exceeded five hundred thousand, making it second only to New York.

Although Philadelphia remained the largest city in the state, Harrisburg became Pennsylvania's capital in 1812 (shown is the State Capitol).

## Changing Lifestyles

Pennsylvania's population continued to grow at a rate of about 30 percent each decade during the early 1800s. Although the state contained unsettled land after the Revolution, by 1840 the frontier was gone as new settlers arrived and built farms and towns. As in colonial days, these newcomers represented diverse religions, cultures, and nationalities.

In some rural areas, farm life was much the same as before the war and was often difficult. Many settlers still built log houses and barns, hunted for food, and made their own clothing and tools. Some people were isolated and had to travel miles to reach a gristmill, school, or general store. Roads in certain areas were rough, especially in mountainous western Pennsylvania. Indian attacks remained a threat during the early 1800s but ended after the remaining Native Americans moved west or to Canada.

Other farmers, especially in southeastern Pennsylvania, were more prosperous and could even afford to hire laborers and other servants. A visitor to that region in the 1830s praised the green fields with "substantial houses, most of which are both handsome and commodious, painted in foreign style" and the "spacious and solidly constructed"[36] barns.

Author of *Thoughts upon Female Education*, Benjamin Rush believed that women could better prepare their children for adulthood if they received an education.

During colonial days, the rural population had always exceeded that of the cities, but after the Revolution the state's urban areas experienced the most rapid growth. In 1790, 90 percent of Pennsylvanians lived in rural areas; by 1860 that figure was 69 percent. As a result, more people had access to urban institutions, including schools and the opportunities and upward mobility that an education could provide.

A free public education system developed after the war. Political leader and physician Benjamin Rush had long promoted this cause for girls as well as for boys. In his influential 1787 book *Thoughts upon Female Education,* Rush contended that education was vital to help women fulfill their roles as mothers who would raise virtuous citizens. In 1790 the state constitution required communities to provide free education to children of both genders whose parents could not afford it.

As time went on, more middle-class parents chose to send their children to nonsectarian schools rather than to the church-affiliated ones that had long taught young Pennsylvanians. Some communities founded neighborhood schools for all children, hired teachers, and then charged a small fee for each pupil. By 1830 one-room schoolhouses could be found all over Pennsylvania. During the decade that followed, state legislators passed a general education law that set up a public school system funded by local taxes and run by local school districts.

These changes improved opportunities for many young Pennsylvanians, but others were left out because of their race. Although slavery was banned in the state, many blacks lived in poverty, and concerned Pennsylvanians set out to improve their living conditions and also to fight alongside both blacks and whites for national laws abolishing slavery.

## Opposing Slavery

Although the Constitutional Convention had not agreed to abolish slavery in the United States, Pennsylvania had already done so on March 3, 1780—the first state to take this action. The law, called the Pennsylvania Gradual Abolition Act, provided that any black or mulatto child born in the state as of the date the act was passed would not be "considered as servants for life, or slaves."[37] As a result of the 1780 act, the number of slaves in Pennsylvania was gradually reduced so that, by 1800, fewer than two thousand remained in the state.

Pennsylvania also became a center of antislavery activities organized by Quakers and other reformers. These citizens worked hard after the Revolutionary War to improve the living conditions of former slaves and to promote antislavery laws around the country where the number of slaves exceeded five hundred thousand.

In Philadelphia free blacks formed the Free African Society in 1787. It worked to improve the economic and social conditions for other blacks through education and job opportunities. Richard Allen, a freedman in his late twenties, was a leader of this group and also helped to found the African Methodist Episcopal Church in Philadelphia, which became a center of social and religious activities in the black community.

In 1789 concerned white citizens in Philadelphia formed an organization for the purpose of "the free instruction of orderly Blacks and People of Color."[38] The Pennsylvania Abolition Society also protected fugitive slaves who had fled from their masters and aided free blacks who were being held unlawfully.

Antislavery activities increased during the 1800s, and Pennsylvanians played a major role in helping escaped slaves reach freedom in Canada via the Underground Railroad. Both rural and urban Pennsylvanians operated Underground Railroad stations. After the Civil War, some newly emancipated African Americans returned to Pennsylvania, where they found work in its thriving industries.

## The Growth of Cities and Industrial Development

During the early 1800s new towns developed in central and western Pennsylvania, often as centers of industrial growth. Only five places—Philadelphia, Lancaster, Chester, Bethlehem, and Reading—were classified as true cities in 1800, and all five were in the east. By 1860 forty-six cities were sprinkled throughout the state, and that number grew during the late 1800s.

One of these growing cities was Pittsburgh, located in western Pennsylvania. Pittsburgh, which was a frontier town of fifteen hundred people in 1800, grew to nearly seventy-eight thousand in 1860. A visitor described this noisy, industrial city in 1831: "The houses and the tremendous factories are wrapped in smoke; in streets and on the

The iron industry was the first large-scale industry in America and became increasingly important as locomotives became a major form of transportation during the 1800s. Pictured is an early iron foundry.

wharves a tumult of . . . carts; everywhere scenes of loading and unloading; iron foundries and the humming of factories." [39]

In Pittsburgh, as elsewhere in the state, industry became an increasingly important segment of the economy. Timber for shipbuilding and paper mills remained important after the war, but iron expanded tremendously. The iron industry was also the first large-scale industry in colonial America, and it became even more important during the 1800s, when iron was needed for new machines and to build locomotives for the rail industry.

Several ironworks were already operating by 1780. Between 1716 and 1729, Thomas Rutter had built Colebrookdale, an iron-making plantation, in Chester County. The Durham Iron Works was founded in 1728 in Bucks County. Within twenty years, the large new Cornwall Furnace was built. During the Revolutionary War, iron from the colony's blast furnaces had produced cannons and other military supplies. Now they focused on peacetime products, such as hardware, tools, and farming implements. They made sheet iron, bar iron, and nails for building. Durham Furnace and Hopewell Furnace, which began operating in 1771, operated in eastern Pennsylvania.

After the war, new ironworks sprang up farther west. The first factory built west of the Allegheny Mountains was Alliance Furnace, constructed in 1789 on Jacob's Creek. During the next seventy years, two hundred more blast furnaces would be constructed in western Pennsylvania.

Furnaces were located in rural areas near places where iron deposits, limestone, and charcoal could all be found. Men heated iron ore with charcoal made from heating logs with hot coals. Waterpower was also vital, so the furnaces were usually placed in valleys or ravines. Villages developed around ironworks, which boosted the economy and provided jobs. One hundred or more people often worked in each factory.

New sources of wealth would be discovered in the form of oil deposits and stores of anthracite and bituminous coal, which provided sources of energy both inside and outside the state. Mining, drilling, and the iron and steel industries would fuel the state's economy into the twentieth century.

Along with mining, drilling, and the iron industry, the steel industry, like this one in Homestead, in 1900, boosted the economy and provided jobs for many Pennsylvanians.

Diversity continued to be a major feature of the state as immigrants came to work in coal mines, steel mills, and other industrial jobs. These people would come from southern and eastern Europe as well as from countries that had been represented in colonial days.

Even with all of its industry and growing population, the state named "Penn's Woods" remained largely forested, and more than half of the state was still covered with trees in the year 2000. Rural farms still dot the landscape, some of them dating back to the 1700s. Vivid reminders of colonial history and the people who made that history can be seen in Philadelphia, Germantown, Bethlehem, and Valley Forge. Through its many economic, political, social, literary, and scientific contributions, Pennsylvania has fulfilled its founder's expectations to become "the seed of a nation."

# Notes

## Introduction: "The Seed of a Nation"

1. Quoted in Sylvester K. Stevens, *Pennsylvania: Birthplace of a Nation.* New York: Random House, 1964, p. 31.

## Chapter One: A Welcoming Land

2. Quoted in Louis B. Wright, *The American Heritage History of the Thirteen Colonies.* New York: American Heritage, 1967, p. 124.
3. Quoted in Stevens, *Pennsylvania,* p. 27.
4. Quoted in Wright, *The American Heritage History of the Thirteen Colonies,* p. 147.

## Chapter Two: William Penn's "Holy Experiment"

5. David Freeman Hawke, *Everyday Life in Early America.* New York: Harper and Row, 1988, p. 229.
6. Quoted in Hawke, *Everyday Life in Early America,* p. 231.
7. Quoted in Jim Powell, "William Penn, America's First Great Champion of Liberty and Peace," *Freeman.* www.quaker.org/wmpenn.html.
8. Quoted in Hawke, *Everyday Life in Early America* , p. 25.
9. William Penn, *First Frame of Government, May 5,* 1682. The Avalon Project at Yale Law School. www.yale.edu/lawweb/avalon/states/pa04.htm.
10. Quoted in Philadelphia Yearly Meeting, "Penn's Holy Experiment: The Seed of a Nation," *Quakers and the Political Process.* www.pym.org/exhibit/p078.html.
11. Quoted in Powell, "William Penn, America's First Great Champion of Liberty and Peace."
12. Quoted in Philadelphia Yearly Meeting, "Penn's Holy Experiment."
13. Quoted in Hans Fantel, *William Penn: Apostle of Dissent.* New York: William Morrow, 1974, p. 185.
14. Quoted in Milton Meltzer, *Ain't Gonna Study War No More.* New York: Harper and Row, 1985, p. 35.
15. Quoted in John W. Kleiner and Helmut T. Lehman, *The Correspondence of Heinrich Melchior Mühlenberg.* Vol. 1. *1740–1747.* Camden, ME: Picton, 1986, p. 118.

16. Quoted in Sanderson Beck, "George Fox, William Penn, and Friends." www.san.beck.org/WP12-FoxandPenn.html.

## Chapter Three: Life in the Pennsylvania Colony
17. Quoted in Stevens, *Pennsylvania*, p. 78.
18. Quoted in Arthur M. Schlesinger Sr. and Dixon Ryan Fox, *A History of American Life*. New York: Simon and Schuster, 1987, p. 191.
19. Quoted in Marshall B. Davidson, *Five Hundred Years of Life in America: An Illustrated History*. New York: Harry N. Abrams, 1982, pp. 43–44.
20. Quoted in Fantel, *William Penn*, p. 173.

## Chapter Four: Revolutionary Years
21. John C. Miller, *This New Man, the American: The Beginnings of the American People*. New York: McGraw-Hill, 1974, p. 617.
22. Quoted in *The War from This Side: Editorials from the "North American."* Vol. 4. www.qhpress.org/quakerpages/qwhp/ww1naed.htm.
23. John Dickinson, "Letters from a Farmer." http://odur.let.rug.nl/~usa/D/1751-1775/townshend/dickII.htm.
24. Quoted in Henry Steele Commager and Richard B. Morris, eds., *The Spirit of 'Seventy-Six: The Story of the American Revolution as Told by Participants*. New York: Bonanza Books, 1983, p. 21.
25. Quoted in Joseph E. Illick, *Colonial Pennsylvania: A History*. New York: Scribner, 1976, p. 227.
26. Quoted in Commager and Morris, *The Spirit of 'Seventy-Six*, pp. 95–96.
27. Quoted in Commager and Morris, *The Spirit of 'Seventy-Six*, p. 282.
28. Thomas Paine, *Common Sense*. www.constitution.org/civ/comsense.htm.
29. Quoted in Illick, *Colonial Pennsylvania*, p. 293.
30. Quoted in Roland M. Baummann, "The Pennsylvania Revolution." www.ushistory.org/pennsylvania/birth2.html.
31. Quoted in Richard Alan Ryerson, *The Revolution Is Now Begun: The Radical Committees of Philadelphia, 1765–1776*. Philadelphia: University of Pennsylvania Press, 1978, p. 236.
32. Quoted in Thomas Paine, *The Crisis: December 23, 1776*. http:www.ushistory.org/paine/crisis/c-01.htm.
33. Quoted in Susan Coolidge, *A Short History of the City of Philadelphia, from Its Foundation to the Present Time, 1871*. Boston: Roberts Brothers, 1887, p. 189.

## Chapter Five: A Dynamic New State

34. Quoted in Clarence P. Hornung, *The Way It Was in the USA: A Pictorial Panorama of America.* New York: Abbeville, 1978, p. 211.
35. Quoted in Stevens, *Pennsylvania,* p. 124.
36. Quoted in Stevens, *Pennsylvania,* p. 124.
37. "An Act for the Gradual Abolition of Slavery, 1780." www.yale.edu/lawweb/avalon/states/pa/pennst01.htm.
38. Quoted in Schlesinger and Fox, *A History of American Life,* p. 385.
39. Quoted in Stevens, *Pennsylvania,* p. 125.

# Chronology

**1609**
Explorer Henry Hudson sails into Delaware Bay.

**1638**
Swedish settlers found New Sweden on the Delaware River.

**1643**
Governor Johan Printz moves the settlement to Tinicum Island, within the boundaries of present-day Pennsylvania.

**1681**
William Penn is granted Pennsylvania by King Charles II of England and lower Delaware by the duke of York.

**1682**
Penn arrives in his colony.

**1683**
Penn buys land from local Native Americans; Quakers and Mennonites found Germantown.

**1685**
Philadelphia becomes the capital of the colony.

**1688**
Colonists in Germantown are the first Americans to formally protest slavery.

**1701**
Penn gives his Charter of Privileges to the colony of Pennsylvania.

**1740**
The first university in Pennsylvania is founded in Philadelphia.

**1755–1763**
French and Indian Wars.

**1774**
The First Continental Congress convenes in Philadelphia.

**1775**
The Second Continental Congress convenes in Philadelphia.

**1776**
The Declaration of Independence is signed in Philadelphia.

**1777**
The British win the Battle of Brandywine and occupy
Philadelphia; the Continental Congress, having relocated to
York, writes the Articles of Confederation; Washington's troops
are defeated in the Battle of Germantown.

**1777–1778**
Washington's army endures the winter at Valley Forge,
Pennsylvania.

**1778**
British troops leave Philadelphia; the Continental Congress returns
to the city.

**1780**
Pennsylvania passes the first law banning slavery in the colonies.

**1783**
The Treaty of Paris is signed, officially ending the Revolutionary
War; Benjamin Franklin continues to serve in France as U.S.
minister.

**1787**
The Constitutional Convention meets in Philadelphia to draft
the U.S. Constitution; Pennsylvania becomes the second state,
after Delaware, to ratify the Constitution.

**1790–1800**
Philadelphia serves as the capital of the United States.

**1791**
The First Bank of the United States is placed in Philadelphia.

**1792**
The U.S. Mint is founded in Philadelphia.

# For Further Reading

## Books

Catherine Drinker Bowen, *Miracle at Philadelphia: The Story of the Constitutional Convention.* Boston: Atlantic Monthly/Little, Brown, 1966. A lively history of the people and events surrounding the writing of the U.S. Constitution.

Gene Brown, *Discovery and Settlement: Europe Meets the New World, 1490–1700.* Brookfield, CT: Millbrook, 1993. This book describes the early exploration and first European settlements in North America.

Kieran Doherty, *William Penn: Quaker Colonist.* Brookfield, CT: Millbrook, 1998. This engrossing biography for young people tells the story of Penn's life and his utopian but practical vision for the colony he founded.

Russell Freedman, *Give Me Liberty: The Story of the Declaration of Independence.* New York: Holiday House, 2000. The engrossing description of the events leading to the American Revolution shows how and why the Declaration of Independence was written and its lasting impact. The book includes quotations from journals, essays, speeches, letters, and songs of that era, along with numerous illustrations.

Kathlyn Gay, *Revolutionary War.* Brookfield, CT: Millbrook, 1995. This book shows events leading up to the war for independence from Britain, important events during the war, and the post-Revolutionary period.

Joy Hakim, *Making Thirteen Colonies* and *From Colonies to Country.* New York: Oxford University Press, 1993. The two volumes in a popular series for young people offer colorful accounts of early American social and political life in the colonies and the war leading to an independent United States.

Clarence P. Hornung, *The Way It Was in the USA: A Pictorial Panorama of America.* New York: Abbeville, 1978. A heavily illustrated look at the various states and regions of the United States throughout history, beginning with colonial times.

Deborah Kent, *African-Americans and the Thirteen Colonies*. New York: Childrens Press, 1988. This book describes the lives and achievements of black Americans, both slaves and free, during colonial days.

Benson J. Lossing, *Lives of the Signers*. New York: Wallbuilders, 1995. This text offers detailed profiles of the men who signed the Declaration of Independence.

Milton Meltzer, *Benjamin Franklin: The New American*. New York: Franklin Watts, 1989. A biography of the versatile, self-made man by an award-winning author of nonfiction for young adults.

George Schaun and Virginia Schaun, *Everyday Life in Colonial Maryland, Delaware, Pennsylvania, and Virginia*. Baltimore: University of Maryland Historical Press, 1996. This social history shows daily life in four of the original thirteen colonies; it also describes the importance of agriculture and trade.

Richard Stein, *A Nation Is Born: Rebellion and Independence in America, 1700–1820*. Brookfield, CT: Millbrook, 1993. Shows the growth of the colonies and their struggle for more freedoms, leading to the Revolutionary War as well as life in the new United States following the war.

Carolyn Kott Washburne, *A Multicultural Portrait of Colonial Life*. New York: Marshall Cavendish, 1994. This text describes life in colonial times from the viewpoint of women and African Americans.

Josh Wilker, *The Lenape Indians*. Broomall, PA: Franklin Watts, 1993. This book describes the history and lifestyles of the Leni-Lenape (Delaware) Indians who lived in the present-day Delaware Valley; written for young people.

Jean Kinney Williams, *The Quakers*. Broomall, PA: Franklin Watts, 1998. A history of the beliefs and social impact of this religious group.

**Websites**

**Africans in America** (www.pbs.org/wgbh/aia/part3/3p248.html). Part three of this Public Broadcasting System series profiles the Quaker antislavery activist Anthony Benezet.

**Anabaptists** (www.anabaptists.org). This website contains the article "U.S. Anabaptists During the Revolutionary War," which describes the activities and pacifist outlook of Anabaptists (and other religious pacifists) during the war.

**Liberty Haven** (www.libertyhaven.com). This website contains articles on various topics, such as democracy and the Constitution. It also contains a historical article on colonial education.

**Life in Mid–Eighteenth Century Pennsylvania** (http://genealogy. about.com/hobbies/genealogy/library/authors/uchumphreyb.htm). This webpage, accessed through the About.com genealogy section, discusses the lives of colonists and new immigrants to Pennsylvania during the mid-1700s; it also includes source notes.

**QuakerPages** (www.qhpress.org/quakerpages). This site contains materials pertaining to Quaker history and religious principles, including first-person accounts of Quakers during the colonial period and the Revolutionary War.

**Slavery in Pennsylvania** (www.geocities.com/Athens/Parthenon/6329). This website contains the article "Text of Pennsylvania's 1780 Act for the Gradual Abolition of Slavery," the first law banning slavery in the colonies or states.

**The Travels of William Bartram** (www.bartramtrail.org). Through this website, readers may access the article "John Bartram, Botanist," a profile of the famous Pennsylvanian who rose from humble roots to help found the American Philosophical Society and become a world-famous botanist.

**ushistory.org** (www.ushistory.org). Created and hosted by the Independence Hall Association, this site contains material on the people and historical events associated with the founding of the United States. The association aims to promote education in the principles of liberty and democratic government that unfolded during the Revolutionary and constitutional periods in Philadelphia.

**The War for American Independence** (http://home.ptd.net/~revwar). Through this website, readers may access the article "The Wyoming Valley Massacre," which describes the massacre of soldiers and civilians at Fort Wyoming, Pennsylvania, during the Revolutionary War.

# Works Consulted

**Books**

Carl and Jessica Bridenbaugh, *Rebels and Gentlemen: Philadelphia in the Age of Franklin*. Westport, CT: Greenwood Press, 1978. This fascinating book focuses on the people who played important roles in the political social development of Philadelphia during colonial and revolutionary times.

Merle Burke, *United States History: The Growth of Our Land*. Chicago: American Technical Society, 1959. An educational text designed for teachers that describes the major events in American history, beginning with colonial times and concluding with the end of President Dwight Eisenhower's administration.

Jon Butler, *Becoming America: The Revolution Before 1776*. Cambridge, MA: Harvard University Press, 2000. A fascinating look at the American colonial experience that shows its diverse settlers, developing economy, and political movements that culminated in the American Revolution.

Henry Steele Commager and Richard B. Morris, eds., *The Spirit of 'Seventy-Six: The Story of the American Revolution as Told by Participants*. New York: Bonanza Books, 1983. Contains nearly one thousand dramatic first-person accounts relating to different aspects of the American Revolution in the various colonies, woven together by narrative writing by the editors. Chapter 14 contains documents related to the British invasion of Philadelphia during the Revolution.

Susan Coolidge, *A Short History of the City of Philadelphia, from Its Foundation to the Present Time, 1871*. Boston: Roberts Brothers, 1887. Coolidge's early history of Pennsylvania examines colonization and the growth and development of Philadelphia from the late 1600s to 1871.

Elaine Forman Crane, ed., *The Diary of Elizabeth Drinker*. Vol. 1: *1758–1795*. Boston: Northeastern University Press, 1991. A fascinating account of daily life in the colonial and Revolutionary War periods from the viewpoint of a Quaker woman in Philadelphia, Elizabeth Sandwith Drinker (1735–1807).

Marshall B. Davidson, *Five Hundred Years of Life in America: An Illustrated History*. New York: Harry N. Abrams, 1982. This heavily illustrated book provides first-person accounts of scenes and people in American history.

William Henry Egle, *History of the Counties of Dauphin and Lebanon in the Commonwealth of Pennsylvania: Biographical and Genealogical*. Salem, MA: Higginson, 1991. This reprint of an 1883 book, written by a prominent historian and genealogist, describes colonial life in two countries.

Hans Fantel, *William Penn: Apostle of Dissent*. New York: William Morrow, 1974. A readable but authoritative biography of Pennsylvania's idealistic Quaker founder, whose utopian vision of a "holy experiment" in America influenced the legal framework of the nation as well as one colony.

Eric Foner, ed., *Thomas Paine: Collected Writings*. New York: Library of America, 1995. This collection includes a biography of Paine, along with his most famous revolutionary works—*Common Sense, The Crisis, Rights of Man, The Age of Reason*—and hundreds of letters, articles, and essays.

Henry Harbough, *Life of Michael Schlatter*. Temecula, CA: Reprint Services Corporation, 1992. A biography of the German clergyman who came to Pennsylvania in 1751 to help unite some of the German religious groups.

David Hawke, *The Colonial Experience*. Indianapolis: Bobbs-Merrill, 1966. This text describes the socioeconomic and religious factors that led Europeans to leave for the American colonies; separate chapters show who settled in each colony and how the government and lifestyles evolved.

David Freeman Hawke, *Everyday Life in Early America*. New York: Harper and Row, 1988. This book describes how the early colonists lived—home and family, occupations, and community activities.

Joseph E. Illick, *Colonial Pennsylvania: A History.* New York: Scribner, 1976. A scholarly look at the development of the Pennsylvania colony, emphasizing political development, including the changing leadership in the colony.

Stanley N. Katz and John M. Murrin, *Colonial America: Essays in Politics and Social Development.* New York: Knopf, 1983. A scholarly account of how people lived in specific ethnic communities in early America; includes a description of Quaker settlements in Pennsylvania with demographics.

John W. Kleiner and Helmut T. Lehman, *The Correspondence of Heinrich Melchior Mühlenberg.* Vol. 1. *1740–1747.* Camden, ME: Picton, 1986. This collection features letters from the Lutheran clergyman who supported colonization of German Lutherans in Pennsylvania and who served that religious community during colonial days.

Milton Meltzer, *Ain't Gonna Study War No More.* New York: Harper and Row, 1985. A history of pacifism and resistance to war, primarily in the United States; it describes Quaker pacifism in colonial days and during the Revolutionary War.

John C. Miller, *This New Man, the American: The Beginnings of the American People.* New York: McGraw-Hill, 1974. This book describes the founding of the various colonies and their development as settlers and black African slaves joined Native Americans to make a new nation with new religious, political, economic, social, and philosophical attitudes.

Phillips Moulton, ed., *The Journal and Major Essays of John Woolman.* Philadelphia: Friends United Press, 1997. This reprint of John Woolman's journal and major essays describes his work to end slavery and his efforts to inspire others to live in peace and simplicity.

John Punshon, *A Portrait in Grey: A Short History of the Quakers.* London: Quaker Home Service, 1999. This look at the development of the Society of Friends discusses the group's founder, George Fox, as well as its roots, philosophy, and activities.

Sarah R. Riedman and Clarence C. Green, *Benjamin Rush: Physician, Patriot, Founding Father.* London: Abelard-Schuman, 1964. A portrait of the famous eighteenth-century physician and statesman who signed the Declaration of Independence and worked to reform care for the mentally ill.

Malcolm J. Rohrbough, *The Trans-Appalachian Frontier.* New York: Oxford University Press, 1978. Describes frontier life west of the Appalachians from the late 1700s into the early 1800s; shows how people formed relationships with their neighbors to survive and build communities.

Richard Alan Ryerson, *The Revolution Is Now Begun: The Radical Committees of Philadelphia, 1765–1776.* Philadelphia: University of Pennsylvania Press, 1978. A fascinating account of the revolutionary political movement in Pennsylvania, which led to a grassroots effort to replace the pacifist-dominated assembly with a unique new legislature composed of men who supported independence.

Arthur M. Schlesinger Sr. and Dixon Ryan Fox, *A History of American Life.* New York: Simon and Schuster, 1987. An acclaimed history focusing on the way people lived in America from the earliest white settlements through the Great Depression; includes many primary sources.

Sylvester K. Stevens, *Pennsylvania: Birthplace of a Nation.* New York: Random House, 1964. A detailed history of Pennsylvania, beginning with Native Americans living there during the century before Europeans arrived. The author shows how the colony and the state of Pennsylvania influenced the development of the United States.

Carl Van Doren, *Benjamin Franklin.* New York: Viking, 1938. A major biography of the self-made early American writer, scientist, diplomat, and statesman who has been called one of the most talented people in history.

Louis B. Wright, *The American Heritage History of the Thirteen Colonies.* New York: American Heritage, 1967. A highly readable and comprehensive look at the development of all thirteen colonies and the American Revolution, with first-person accounts and photographs.

## Periodicals

Gordon Young, "Pennsylvania, Faire Land of William Penn," *National Geographic*, June 1978. A pictorial article showing the land and people of Pennsylvania in the late seventies; includes historical background and quotes from William Penn and other colonists.

## Internet Sources

"An Act for the Gradual Abolition of Slavery, 1780." http://www.yale.edu/lawweb/avalon/states/pa/pennst01.htm.

Roland M. Baummann, "The Pennsylvania Revolution." www.ushistory.org/pennsylvania/birth2.html.

Sanderson Beck, "George Fox, William Penn, and Friends." www.san.beck.org/WP12-FoxandPenn.html.

John Dickinson, "Letters from a Farmer." http://odur.let.rug.nl/~usa/D/1751-1775/townshend/dickII.htm.

Thomas Paine, *Common Sense*. www.constitution.org/civ/comsense.htm.

William Penn, *First Frame of Government, May 5, 1682*. The Avalon Project at Yale School. www.yale.edu/lawweb/avalon/states/pa04.htm.

Philadelphia Yearly Meeting, "Penn's Holy Experiment: The Seed of a Nation," *Quakers and the Political Process*. www.pym.org/exhibit.p078.html.

Jim Powell, "William Penn, America's First Great Champion of Liberty and Peace," *Freeman*. www.quaker.org/wmpenn.html.

Albigence Waldo, "From the Diary of Albigence Waldo, Surgeon at Valley Forge, 1777." http://odur.let.rug.nl/~usa/D/1776-1800/war/waldo.htm.

*The War from This Side: Editorials from the "North American."* Vol. 4. www.qhpress.org/quakerpages/qwhp/ww1naed.htm.

# Index

# Index

industry
   first large scale industry in U.S., 75
   growth of, 73–77
   iron, 34
   textiles, 41–42, 52
   waterpower and, 75
Ireland, 24
Iroquois Indians, 12

Jacob's Creek, 75
James, duke of York, 20
Jamestown, Virginia, 15, 20
Jefferson, Thomas, 57
Jews, 32–33
*Journal and Essays of John Woolman, The*
   (Woolman), 39
Junto clubs, 39

Karsholm, 18
King George's War, 50

Lackawanna River, 11
Lancaster
   Congress moved to, 61
   founded, 31–32
   industrial growth and, 73
   on overland trade route, 44
Lancaster County, 45
Lancaster Turnpike, 56
Lehigh River, 11
Lenape River, 15
   *see also* Delaware River
Leni-Lenape Indians, 12, 16
   treaty with, 30–31
*Letters from a Farmer in Pennsylvania to the*
   *Inhabitants of the British Colonies*
   (Dickinson), 52
Lexington, Massachusetts, 55
Liberty Bell, 66
Lion's Inn, 23
Loe, Thomas, 24
Logan, Deborah
   on battle near Germantown, 62
Louis XIV (king of France), 61
Luther, Martin, 32
Lutheranism, 18, 32

Madison, James, 69
Maryland, 20
Massachusetts Bay (Massachusetts), 20
Matlock, Timothy, 60
Maur, Christopher, 33
men
   clothing of, 37, 41
   Junto clubs and, 39

   in rural area, 40
   social life of, 46
Mennonites
   immigration and, 31, 32
   pacifism and, 60
   slavery and, 39
Mifflin, Thomas, 54, 60
military
   establishment of militia, 58
   pacifism and, 50
   privations of, 58–59
   at Valley Forge, 63
   veterans' pay and, 67–68
Miller, John C.
   on Indian policy, 49
Minuit, Peter, 16
Miranda, Isaac, 32
Mississippi River, 11
Monongahela Indians, 12
Monoshone Creek, 32
Moravians, 32, 60
Morris, Gouverneur, 69
Morton, John, 57

Nanticoke Indians, 12
Native Americans, 12–15
   agriculture, 12–15
   allies to Europeans, 49
   attacks by, 50, 71
   civil rights of, 8–9
   disease and, 14
   dwellings of, 12
   Europeans and, 14–16
   French Indian Wars and, 50
   lifestyle of, 12–15
   maize and, 13
   vanished from Pennsylvania, 65
   William Penn and, 30–31
natural resources
   abundance of, 11
   described by Hudson, 15
   industry and, 75
   rich soil as, 7
New England, 20
New Gothenburg, 17
New Hampshire, 20
New Jersey, 61
New Netherland, 16, 20
New Sweden, 16
   capital of, 17
   malnutrition, 18
New Sweden Company, 17
New York (state), 11–12, 16
New York City, 44, 61–62
   as U.S. capital, 69

93

# Picture Credits

Cover photo: Superstock

© CORBIS, 23, 71, 72

© CORBIS/Bettmann, 30

© CORBIS/Lee Snider, 19

© CORBIS/Joseph Sohm; Visions of America, 66

Hulton/Archive by Getty Images, 8, 10, 16, 25, 26, 35, 38, 54, 56, 64, 69, 76

Library of Congress, 45, 57, 59, 68

North Wind Pictures, 13, 14, 17, 27, 28, 31, 36, 38 (inset), 41, 43, 44, 47, 51, 52, 53, 60, 67, 74

# About the Author

Victoria Sherrow holds B.S. and M.S. degrees from Ohio State University. Among her writing credits are numerous stories and articles, ten books of fiction, and more than fifty books of nonfiction for children and young adults. Her recent books have explored such topics as biomedical ethics, the Great Depression, and the Holocaust. For Lucent Books, she has written *The Titanic, Life During the Gold Rush,* and *The Righteous Gentiles.* Sherrow lives in Connecticut with her husband, Peter Karoczkai, and their three children.